Gaining from Migration

TOWARDS A NEW MOBILITY SYSTEM

by
Jeff Dayton-Johnson, Louka T. Katseli, Gregory Maniatis,
Rainer Münz and Demetrios Papademetriou

OECD

DEVELOPMENT CENTRE OF THE ORGANISATION
FOR ECONOMIC CO-OPERATION AND DEVELOPMENT

ORGANISATION FOR ECONOMIC CO-OPERATION AND DEVELOPMENT

The OECD is a unique forum where the governments of 30 democracies work together to address the economic, social and environmental challenges of globalisation. The OECD is also at the forefront of efforts to understand and to help governments respond to new developments and concerns, such as corporate governance, the information economy and the challenges of an ageing population. The Organisation provides a setting where governments can compare policy experiences, seek answers to common problems, identify good practice and work to co-ordinate domestic and international policies.

The OECD member countries are: Australia, Austria, Belgium, Canada, the Czech Republic, Denmark, Finland, France, Germany, Greece, Hungary, Iceland, Ireland, Italy, Japan, Korea, Luxembourg, Mexico, the Netherlands, New Zealand, Norway, Poland, Portugal, the Slovak Republic, Spain, Sweden, Switzerland, Turkey, the United Kingdom and the United States. The Commission of the European Communities takes part in the work of the OECD.

OECD Publishing disseminates widely the results of the Organisation's statistics gathering and research on economic, social and environmental issues, as well as the conventions, guidelines and standards agreed by its members.

Also available in French under the title:
Faire des migrations un atout
POUR UN NOUVEAU SYSTÈME DE MOBILITÉ

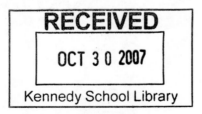

Corrigenda to OECD publications may be found on line at: *www.oecd.org/publishing/corrigenda*.

© OECD 2007

THE DEVELOPMENT CENTRE

The Development Centre of the Organisation for Economic Co-operation and Development was established by decision of the OECD Council on 23 October 1962 and comprises 22 member countries of the OECD: Austria, Belgium, the Czech Republic, Finland, France, Germany, Greece, Iceland, Ireland, Italy, Korea, Luxembourg, Mexico, the Netherlands, Norway, Portugal, Slovak Republic, Spain, Sweden, Switzerland, Turkey and the United Kingdom as well as Brazil since March 1994, Chile since November 1998, India since February 2001, Romania since October 2004, Thailand since March 2005 and South Africa since May 2006. The Commission of the European Communities also takes part in the Centre's Governing Board.

The Development Centre, whose membership is open to both OECD and non-OECD countries, occupies a unique place within the OECD and in the international community. Members finance the Centre and serve on its Governing Board, which sets the biennial work programme and oversees its implementation.

The Centre links OECD members with developing and emerging economies and fosters debate and discussion to seek creative policy solutions to emerging global issues and development challenges. Participants in Centre events are invited in their personal capacity.

A small core of staff works with experts and institutions from the OECD and partner countries to fulfil the Centre's work programme. The results are discussed in informal expert and policy dialogue meetings, and are published in a range of high-quality products for the research and policy communities. The Centre's *Study Series* presents in-depth analyses of major development issues; *Policy Briefs* and *Policy Insights* summarise major conclusions for policy makers; *Working Papers* deal with the more technical aspects of the Centre's work.

For an overview of the Centre's activities, please see www.oecd.org/dev

Foreword

An increasingly central dimension of globalisation is human mobility. Policy makers and citizens look with growing interest — and sometimes with alarm — upon the link between this emerging mobility system and economic and social outcomes of migrant-sending and migrant-receiving countries. Can international migration contribute to economic progress? Almost certainly; at present, however, the prospects for gaining from migration are beset by a variety of institutional obstacles. Migrants themselves, by and large, certainly gain from their mobility, relative to staying home; but they could conceivably benefit even more under a reformed migration management regime. The costs and benefits of their mobility to the societies to which they move, and which they leave behind, are more complicated still.

This publication synthesises the conclusions of several background reports prepared for the "Gaining from Migration" project regarding key dimensions of the new labour mobility system: the impact of immigration on employment, wages and economic growth; the lessons from Europe's experiences with integration of immigrants; the impact of emigration on economic development in low and middle income migrant-sending countries; and the role of diaspora networks. The result is a report that makes concrete recommendations for policy innovations in migrant receiving and migrant sending countries alike.

ISBN: 978-92-64-03740-3 © OECD 2007

Acknowledgements

This document is a synthesis of the results of the Gaining from Migration project. It is based on inputs provided by the members of the project team, who produced a number of critical evaluative reviews, working papers, policy briefs and case studies for the project. The authors drew equally upon the work and collaborative energy of additional experts associated with the project: Betsy Cooper and Sarah Spencer (COMPAS, University of Oxford); Anna di Mattia and Theodora Xenogiani (OECD Development Centre); Robert E.B. Lucas, Jr. (Boston University); Marco Martiniello (Université de Liège); Doris Meissner (Migration Policy Institute); Rinus Penninx, Jan Rath and Aimee Rindoks (IMES, University of Amsterdam); and Thomas Straubhaar, Florin Vadean and Nan Vadean (Hamburgisches Weltwirtschafts Institut). The complete list of authors and outputs can be found in the Annex.

Special thanks go to members of the Project Steering Committee, most notably Antonis Kastrissianakis and Xavier Prats Monné (former and current Directors, respectively, of the Directorate General for Employment, Social Affairs and Equal Opportunities of the European Commission), Germana Ricciardi and Constantinos Fotakis from the European Commission and John Martin, Director, Jean-Pierre Garson, and Georges Lemaître from the Directorate of Employment, Labour and Social Affairs of the OECD.

This report has also benefited from the valuable insights of an informal Advisory Board consisting of Joaquín Arango (Universidad Complutense), Ibrahim Awad (International Labour Organization), Claude Bébéar (AXA France), Denise Charlton (Immigrant Council of Ireland), Guillaume Cruse (Agence Française de Développement), Bibek Debroy (Chamber of Commerce and Industry, India), Rui Marques (High Commissioner for Immigration and Ethnic Minorities, Portugal), Piaras Macéinrí (Department of Geography, University College of Cork, Ireland), Claude Moraes (European Parliament), Dilip Ratha (The World Bank), Meera Sethi (International Organization for Migration), Nand Kishore Singh (Global Commission on International Migration), Rita Süssmuth (Global Commission on International Migration) and Alexandros Zavos (President, Hellenic Migration Policy Institute).

Moreover the report has benefited from the comments of other participants in the three experts' meetings organised on 10/11 January 2006, 11 July 2006 and 23 March 2007, and at a conference entitled Migration and Development: A Euro-Mediterranean Perspective, organised by the OECD Development Centre and the Hellenic Migration Policy Institute.

We extend our acknowledgements to external and internal reviewers: Nicholas Glytsos (KEPE); Hania Zlotnik and Bela Hovy (UN Department of Economic and Social Affairs, Population Division) and Javier Santiso (OECD Development Centre).

Completion of the Gaining from Migration project would not have been possible without generous financial and operational support from the European Commission for which the OECD Development Centre expresses its gratitude. A number of OECD member countries also contributed to the Centre's activities on Policy Coherence and Migration and their participation is gratefully acknowledged.

The volume has been edited by Jeff Dayton-Johnson (OECD Development Centre) and Wanda Ollis (external editor). Vanda Legrandgérard (OECD Development Centre's Publications and Media Unit) transformed the manuscript into the publication.

ISBN: 978-92-64-03740-3 © OECD 2007

Table of Contents

ISBN: 978-92-64-03740-3 © OECD 2007

Preface

An increasingly central dimension of globalisation is human mobility. The foreign-born population in OECD countries is approximately 8 per cent, reflecting a dramatic rise over recent decades. Policy makers and citizens look with growing interest — and sometimes with alarm — upon the economic and social consequences of these trends for OECD countries, migrants' countries of origin, and the migrants themselves. Can international migration contribute to economic progress?

The *Gaining from Migration* project, co-ordinated by the OECD Development Centre and supported by the Directorate for Employment, Social Affairs and Equal Opportunities of the European Commission, brought together a broad network of experts to assess what we know about international migration to European countries, economic and social integration experiences in Europe, the role of diasporas, and the migration-development connection in migrants' home countries. A wide array of studies was produced in various formats, and a fruitful sequence of workshops and conferences was organised (details on all of the project outputs are provided in an Annex to this report and at the project's website: www.oecd.org/dev/migration).

The narrow objective of the present report is to distil the main policy lessons and recommendations from the foregoing work; its broader goal is to shed light on the ways in which governments can make the emerging global mobility system work better for the benefit of societies of both receiving and sending countries, as well as for migrants. As such, this final project report has a slightly different character from many of the Development Centre's publications: it is essentially a set of policy proposals, aimed mainly at European migrant-receiving countries, but also at their developing-country partners. While we have rigorously provided references and links to other, more detailed project outputs to back up our assertions and recommendations, a full account of the underlying research and analyses will not be found between these covers.

ISBN: 978-92-64-03740-3 © OECD 2007

Furthermore, this report's recommendations are not those of the OECD, its Development Centre, the EU, or any of the member countries of those organisations. Instead, these proposals are offered by the five leading members of the Core Project Team. Our goal is to promote discussion that will lead the players in the emerging world migration system to forge meaningful mobility partnerships, partnerships to generate more, and more equitably shared, gains for all parties. The next step is to bring these parties to the table and begin to form a consensus; it is our hope that this report will help inspire them to do so.

Louka T. Katseli
Director
OECD Development Centre
July 2007

ISBN: 978-92-64-03740-3 © OECD 2007

Executive Summary
A Set of Migration Policy Proposals for Europe

Europe will, on current trends, come to rely ever more on immigrants to balance supply and demand in labour markets, and more generally to fuel economic growth, as spelled out in the European Union's Lisbon Agenda. International migration to Europe likewise has the potential to promote economic development in the migrants' countries of origin, thereby serving European countries' development co-operation objectives as well.

New Migration Thinking for a New Century (Chapter 2)

Contrary to conventional wisdom, the goals of the key stakeholders in international migration — societies of origin, destination and migrants themselves — are not necessarily at odds. To be sure, there are trade-offs, but partnerships among the players promise better capacity to maximise the benefits and reduce the risks associated with international migration. In pursuit of meaningful partnerships, governments in migrant sending and receiving countries alike must undertake difficult policy reforms, and they must also, in consultation with their constituents, develop new ways of thinking about the migration phenomenon. In many cases, policy reform and rebuilding public confidence will work hand in hand: for example, combating illegal and irregular migration is a necessary policy objective, but will simultaneously recapture control of how European public opinion perceives the migration process.

On the basis of the extensive analysis of the Gaining from Migration project, this report lays out a set of policy proposals that can help European countries and migrants' countries of origin alike to reform the management of the emerging labour mobility system. The report makes detailed proposals in four general domains: policies for European labour markets; policies for social integration of immigrants in Europe; development co-operation policies

ISBN: 978-92-64-03740-3 © OECD 2007

that affect migrants' countries of origin; and initiatives for encouraging and mobilising diaspora networks.

Our general message is that the new system should not be thought of as an *immigration* system at all: instead, it should be conceptualised as an emerging system of international labour mobility. Those that govern the new mobility system should be willing to shape it. Specifically, they need to:

— make clear to migrants what is expected of them and what they can expect;

— be willing to explain the logic and rationale of immigration policies to the electorate and defend the new system against its detractors;

— engage with migrants and their countries of origin as genuine partners in governing the mobility system; and

— be willing to adjust immigration postures to reflect both changing circumstances and the results from ongoing evaluations.

Migration and Employment: Labour Market Access Policies (Chapter 3)

The demand for labour provided by both highly and low- or semi- skilled immigrants will likely continue to increase in Europe. These different types of migration call for a range of policies governing access to European labour markets — policies that must be transparent, responsive and cohesive.

This report makes four sets of proposals related to labour-market access.

— First, a new mobility system will require the development of an integrated migration monitoring system to provide effective monitoring of flows. Only then can those migrants and employers who follow the rules be rewarded with continued access to the mobility system.

— Second, labour-market access policies should facilitate circular migration for those workers in critical occupational categories who do not aim for permanent residence.

— Third, harmonisation across Europe must provide uniform access to labour markets in every country, for defined categories of skilled workers.

— Fourth, labour-market and citizenship policies must be attractive to those workers — highly skilled or not — needed in European labour markets and who seek eventually the security and stability of permanent residence and citizenship.

ISBN: 978-92-64-03740-3 © OECD 2007

Migration and Social Cohesion: Enabling Integration (Chapter 4)

During the second half of the 20th century, European countries became increasingly pressed to integrate immigrants into the life of European societies, but the resources devoted to this enterprise were not always sufficient to the task. Today, integration is viewed as the totality of policies and practices that allow societies to close the gap between the performance of natives and immigrants (and their descendants).

Policy makers face three immediate priorities in the pursuit of this goal.

— First, European countries must provide fair and equal access to the labour market at the earliest point in the immigration experience for all migrants and their family members; economic integration is the surest determinant of social integration.

— Second, European countries must provide access to the educational system, and to specialised language and other classes, at the earliest possible stage in the immigration experience for all family members.

— Third, European countries must seek ways to enable the fullest participation of immigrants in the political and social life of their new country.

Migration and Development: Partnerships for Mobility Management (Chapter 5)

Migration to European countries can promote economic and social progress in migrants' home countries, but only if the process is better managed — by European countries, and by the sending countries as well.

In this light, this report makes four general policy recommendations.

— First, European countries must revisit their migration policies with an eye to ensuring that these policies are consistent with their development co-operation goals, and that developing countries derive greater benefits from migration flows.

— Second, developing countries are encouraged to mainstream migration and remittance dimensions into their national development strategies, especially their poverty reduction strategy papers; European countries, in the context of their development co-operation policies, can help build capacity and provide other forms of assistance to developing countries in this area.

ISBN: 978-92-64-03740-3 © OECD 2007

— Third, the organisational structures for migration management must be reformed both at the national and EU levels, in order to promote better mechanisms for communication and consensus building across ministries and directorates.

— Fourth, the EU and its member states should pursue greater coherence across different policy domains and generate greater synergies across migration, trade (including trade in services), security and development policies; this coherence extends, in line with the EU's Consensus on Development, to policies affecting employment, decent work and the social dimensions of globalisation.

Encouraging Diaspora Networks (Chapter 6)

Diaspora networks straddle countries of origin and countries of destination in a meaningful way, and can play a productive role in improving labour market outcomes, promoting social and economic integration, and contributing to economic development in sending countries.

The report makes three concrete proposals regarding diaspora networks.

— Substantial support — financial and technical — should be provided to migrant organisations and networks in a fair and transparent way.

— Migrants' organisations must be incorporated into the policy-making progress to improve labour market, integration and development co-operation policies.

— Co-development policies in particular, which mobilise the resources and skills of members of diaspora networks, should be deepened to improve the effectiveness of development co-operation.

ISBN: 978-92-64-03740-3 © OECD 2007

Chapter 1

Introduction: Jobs and Confidence

Migration is an increasingly central dimension of globalisation. The result is a new mobility system characterised by diverse forms of migration patterns. Policy makers and citizens look with growing interest — and sometimes with alarm — upon the links between this emerging mobility system and the economic and social outcomes within migrant-sending and migrant-receiving countries. Can international migration contribute to economic progress? With appropriate policies and programmes addressing all sectors of societies affected by migration, it can. At present, however, the prospects for economic and other gains from migration are beset by a variety of institutional obstacles.

Migrants generally gain from their mobility, relative to staying home; but they could conceivably benefit even more under a reformed migration management regime. The costs and benefits of their mobility to the societies to which they move, and which they leave behind, are more complicated still.

The desired level and characteristics of immigration should result from strategic decisions made by the societies of the European Union (EU) member states in deliberative fashion. This means each society must consider the trade-offs — lower or higher economic output, greater or lesser diversity, lower or higher pensions, earlier or later retirement, and even more or less cohesion — and decide what level of immigration is right for them. Legal and humanitarian obligations, of course, are also important factors that should shape decisions and constrain the range of options.

Societies will make better choices if they consider the evidence and socio-economic realities. Demagoguery, where it is present, must be rejected as it perpetuates falsehoods, stereotypes, prejudices and doomsday scenarios that are wholly without evidence. They must be wary of incomplete data and selective or otherwise faulty analyses. With these concerns in mind, the Organisation for Economic Co-operation and Development (OECD) Development Centre, the Migration Policy Institute, supported by the European Commission, co-ordinated work by various experts to assess the migration, integration and development landscape in the EU.

This final report is the result of a critical review of the research and policy literature by researchers and policy analysts. Their analyses cover 1 500 pages in 15 separate reports and case studies. Four overviews evaluate the state of knowledge in the European context and provide statistical background information. In addition, four OECD Development Centre Policy Briefs summarise the key findings of these evaluative reports. These documents are all listed in the Annex and can be accessed from the project website. The overriding purpose of this final report is to distil the main policy options and recommendations from the foregoing work with the ultimate goal of making explicit the ways governments can make migration work better for the benefit of migrants and the societies of both receiving and sending countries.

A central focus of this report is jobs. A concern for jobs unites the interests of the three principal actors in the migration system: societies of origin, destination and migrants themselves. The benefits from better employment, which reflects the training and skills of job candidates, will accrue to all the stakeholders within the migration system.

Almost all European countries will experience rapid ageing of their populations and declining workforces in the coming decades. Projections indicate that the size of the native-born work force in Europe will decline by over 16 million by 2025, and by nearly 44 million by 2050[1]. During these decades, high population growth rates in North Africa — Europe's neighbour to the south — are expected to continue far ahead of economic growth. This means that a large cohort of its potential work force will seek work opportunities in Europe and elsewhere. As well, unemployed and under-employed workers from the less advanced economies east of the European Union, many with skills and education, will continue to seek employment opportunities in the EU for the foreseeable future. The realities of an ageing European population and a declining workforce combined with neighbouring countries that have pools of workers seeking gainful employment suggest an obvious conclusion: the EU and its member states need a rational system of orderly, safe and well-regulated labour mobility.

Jobs also lie at the heart of another challenge facing European societies, specifically, the integration of immigrants. Employment is the most important enabler of integration.

ISBN: 978-92-64-03740-3 © OECD 2007

Income from jobs is furthermore a source of benefits that developing countries derive from migration — they feed the vast flow of remittances from the developed to the developing world. Jobs also abet the transfer of skills, technology and knowledge across borders. Moreover, emigration to EU member states can improve job prospects in developing countries for workers who do not migrate.

Finally, the jobs of European nationals are also at the centre of a political debate that concerns possible disadvantages due to increasing competition for jobs. Ensuring that these workers have fair access to fulfilling employment is a prerequisite for successful acceptance by the public of fair and effective migration systems.

For the most part, European countries do not have immigration systems that adequately address their workforce needs. This report is about how policy makers can use evidence-based research to build public confidence in European migration systems. For European migration systems — and societies — to function well in the coming years, policy makers will also have to gain the confidence of all major stakeholders. The people of Europe must believe that the system is indeed manageable — which is not obvious. One indicator: according to the European Commission, between five and 10 million foreign migrants may be working in Europe without proper authorisation to do so[2]. Confidence is a necessary condition for public support for needed reforms.

Jobs and confidence, moreover, are necessary but not sufficient conditions to encourage general acceptance of migrants by the community at large. Promoting general acceptance of migrants is another key element needed in a successful mobility system, particularly in societies not accustomed to welcoming large numbers of foreigners. Returning migrants, frequently the bearers of new ideas and practices gleaned during their sojourns abroad, also need to be accepted back into their societies.

The analysis and recommendations in this report focus on building confidence in the international labour mobility system. The report proposes reforms to help European governments debate and develop legislation related to mobility[3].

ISBN: 978-92-64-03740-3 © OECD 2007

Notes

1. These projections refer to the labour force — not the working-age population — in the EU25 countries, plus the Channel Islands, Iceland, Liechtenstein, Norway and Switzerland. For fuller details of the forecasting exercise, refer to Münz *et al.* (2006*a*), section 4.1 and Table 3.

2. Estimates of the size of the irregular migrant population in Europe come from various sources. Jandl (2004) estimated that the annual flow of irregular migrants into the EU15 countries was 650 000 annually in the early 2000s. The status of nearly 4 million migrants with irregular status was regularised in five EU countries alone since the early 1980s: France, Greece, Italy, Portugal and Spain; the details are provided in the European Commission's "Policy Plan on Legal Migration", (see European Commission, 2005*a*).

3. This is not to say that Europe has been inactive in formulating a new migration framework. An electronic annex detailing Recent Initiatives taken by the European Commission in the area of Migration is available on the OECD Development Centre's Migration and Development website (www.oecd.org/dev/migration).

ISBN: 978-92-64-03740-3 © OECD 2007

Chapter 2

New Migration Thinking for a New Century

The failure to manage the changes wrought by migration may engender social unrest and political instability. Not managing migration furthermore squanders the potential for migration to contribute to a nation's dynamism, growth and prosperity, while thwarting migrants' aspirations.

States everywhere are struggling to respond to the challenges of migration and to avail themselves of its opportunities, including the OECD countries. The efforts of the member states of the EU are complicated by two factors. The first is the legacy of earlier policy choices, particularly their decades-long denial of the permanence of immigration, and the resulting marginalisation of immigrants and their offspring. The second is that migrants to the EU are often effectively beyond the reach of policy makers. For example, many immigration flows are only loosely linked to labour market conditions in EU member states. This is the case of migrants who enter EU member states via non-economic channels, including legally protected family (re)unification legislation or through asylum claims, or migrants who enter legally but remain after their visas expire, as well as those who enter illegally.

Box 2.1 explains discretionary and non-discretionary immigration flows, while Table 2.1 illustrates non-discretionary migration in selected OECD countries (i.e. the levels of economic and non-economic migration flows for selected OECD countries in recent years). These data illustrate the sizeable share of non-economic migrant categories, but also the considerable differences across countries.

ISBN: 978-92-64-03740-3 © OECD 2007

Box 2.1 Discretionary and Non-discretionary Immigration Flows

Not every immigrant in European countries is actively selected (whether by governments or employers), because not all migration is subject to governmental discretion. Even in countries with restrictive migration regimes, some immigrants are admitted because of treaties or conventions. Notably, within the European Union there is free movement for all European Union citizens, with some temporary exceptions facing citizens of some new member states. In addition, recognised asylum seekers are not subject to active selection criteria (although receiving countries sometimes apply asylum policies more or less restrictively). Other immigrants enter in accordance with universally recognised human rights. These include the right to live with one's spouse and children as well as the right to marry or adopt whom one wishes (OECD countries have nevertheless adopted more or less restrictive policies concerning family re-unification).

Table 2.1. **Non-discretionary Migration in Selected OECD Countries, 2003**

	Total permanent immigration	Of which non-discretionary	Components	
			Family + humanitarian	Free movement
	(thousands)	(percentage)	(percentage)	(percentage)
Canada	221	28	28	-
United States	706	39	39	-
France	173	83	61	21
United Kingdom	244	49	23	25
Sweden	41	95	73	22
Switzerland	82	94	31	63

Source: OECD (2006). Total permanent immigration is reported using a harmonised OECD methodology, and thus statistics might differ from those reported by individual countries' statistical offices.

With the potential costs of failure and the benefits from success both so high, it is paramount for EU member states to manage the migration process better through thoughtful regulation and other policy interventions at the local, national, regional, and international levels. Better management of migration means designing a set of institutions that offers more consistent incentives to the stakeholders (migrants, workers in receiving and sending countries, migrants' families, employers, trade unions, and local and national governments) in order to facilitate favourable job outcomes and to improve social acceptance of migrants.

ISBN: 978-92-64-03740-3 © OECD 2007

Political will and effective policies are needed for managing a more orderly and flexibly regulated flow of legal immigrants, and to incorporate them successfully into the society and its institutions. Deliberate management of migration flows, however, must bear in mind the impact of policy and management decisions on migrants' home countries: a successful mobility system should not drain poorer countries of critically needed teachers, doctors, nurses and other specialists, but it should instead expand the incentives offered to emigration and transit countries to work towards a more orderly system.

What's Old and What's New in Migration Thinking

The quest for successful migration management is hindered by lack of knowledge and ill-defined concepts and policy thinking that lead to poor outcomes. For instance, permanent and temporary migration are distinctions that are losing their ability to describe how people behave today — resulting in policies that lock people in (or out). Many permanent immigrants return to their countries or move on to other countries. That process is likely to accelerate as information flows regarding far-flung job opportunities improve and as the costs of migration fall. Similarly, many temporary migrants stay on (legally or illegally) in their countries of employment. These realities demand that the administrators of migration systems become as flexible and adaptable as migrants, their families and their employers. Only then will those who make and interpret the rules make decisions that deliver the policy outcomes an active mobility system requires.

Assuming there are major economic differences among family migration, employment-based, or skills-tested, migration is another area where lack of knowledge affects policy decisions. For states that engage in all forms of migration, the differences in gross labour-market terms are not always as great as assumed. When families migrate, more than one family member usually works, and the members may have skills that span the skills continuum from low to high. Migrants selected on the basis of skills, meanwhile, also often migrate with family members of similar skill levels who will work, and will increasingly do so in the years ahead[1].

Another concept also bears serious examination: the more- versus less-skilled differential is less meaningful than is commonly thought. Where labour is needed, the standard measure of educational or vocational attainment — high-skilled and low-skilled — might be of little relevance. The term "unskilled work" reflects the skill requirements of a job rather than the job-holder's skill capital.

ISBN: 978-92-64-03740-3 © OECD 2007

As shortages and mismatches across the skills spectrum intensify, recognising the human capital of all immigrants so as to employ it more smartly, even strategically, must become a priority. In this regard, we must focus our policies on what have become critical occupational categories in EU labour markets. Some of these, for example in science and medicine, are rightly recognised as highly skilled. Other categories, for example in construction, tourism, or care of the elderly, may not correspond to traditional definitions of skilled work, but they are of value and fill labour force needs. There exist essential segments of EU labour markets in which immigrants increasingly fill real gaps across the entire skills spectrum.

Skill differentials and occupational attainments matter, and will continue to matter, for migrant-sending countries in the developing world. The composition and quality of a migrant's human capital critically affects the economic consequences of his or her mobility on the home country. Therefore, the distinction between low and high skills will continue to be a useful one for sending countries.

A further increasingly outmoded concept is a distinction between sending and receiving countries. Most countries simultaneously send and receive migrants and, increasingly, are corridors through which migrants pass. For instance, the United Kingdom is one of the European Union's largest attraction poles for new migrants. At the same time, it is one of the world's largest emigration countries, with 5.5 million (nearly 10 per cent) of its nationals living abroad (Sriskandarajah and Drew, 2006). Similarly, Poland simultaneously experiences meaningful rates of immigration and emigration. Another example, from a different region, demonstrates the same point. More than 10 per cent of Mexican nationals have emigrated to the United States, the majority illegally. Mexico also hosts more than a million foreign nationals and is a major transit corridor for migrants to the United States (OECD, 2006).

There is also a growing number of transit countries, whose involvement in the international mobility system is intense. Consider, for instance, the case of sub-Saharan Africans in West or North Africa en route to the EU, or indeed mobility of non-EU citizens among various EU member states. Migration corridors — a concept that is gaining currency among experts and is being adopted by policy makers — can have massive economic consequences for local economies, even if the aggregate effects of migration are more difficult to detect at the national level. Most important, migration corridors are a feature of the emergence of genuinely transnational labour markets, which call for transnational partnerships and governance mechanisms to maximise benefits, minimise risks and ensure the protection of workers' rights.

ISBN: 978-92-64-03740-3 © OECD 2007

Old and New Ways of Thinking and Acting on Migration

What are some of the policy consequences of the old thinking on migration? And how might thinking differently in a systematic way change how we conduct our migration business?

The old thinking uses well-worn aphorisms to stop conversations about well-considered openings to immigration. As a result, we fail to ask the questions to which answers must be found. Forward-looking policies become rarer, as do those that promote economic interests while being mindful of social consequences. Consider two related examples. First is the mindless refrain, "nothing is more permanent than a temporary immigrant"; the other is Max Frisch's oft-repeated aphorism, "We asked for workers but people came". Both remarks are intended to give pause to those considering more open migration systems and to embolden immigration sceptics. Today, these comments are less useful than ever as policy guides. Taken literally, such attitudes close off discussion of temporary migration, which denies societies and individuals access to migration, a powerful motor of growth.

Other characteristics of the old thinking similarly discourage new initiatives. The old thinking is static. Migration is an increasingly dynamic phenomenon that cannot be managed with concepts and policy instruments from a different era, and with outmoded ideas about how to manage (read: "protect") labour markets. This kind of static thinking marginalises immigrants and frequently encourages them to join the unofficial economy, rendering their integration more problematic and hampering dynamic efficiency and employment creation. Labour needs are not static and should be evaluated based on the kind of expertise needed at a given time with recognition of the dynamics in both sending and receiving countries.

Consider how the inflexibility of many EU labour markets is reinforced through decisions about immigration. For instance, the individualised labour-market tests still required of employers in some countries before they hire a prospective immigrant are intended, *a priori*, to discourage employers from hiring immigrants. Immigrants in turn, may find their only opportunity for work lies in the underground economy. Labour markets cannot operate effectively if guiding policies and regulations are made independently of demographic changes and market forces. These vestiges of the old thinking assume that the number of jobs in an economy is somehow finite and domestic labour markets thus need to be protected from competition from migrants.

ISBN: 978-92-64-03740-3 © OECD 2007

The old thinking is also seemingly uninterested in migrants' human capital. Accordingly, the old system does not invest thoughtfully in preparing immigrants and their children to succeed in the labour market, and thus often contributes to their economic marginalisation, if only inadvertently; hence the existence of high unemployment rates among immigrants and their descendants in many EU member states, their sporadic employment, and their massive over-representation in low-wage jobs and low-income cohorts. Here, too, the past weighs down the present. By unrealistically expecting that foreigners and their offspring would somehow return to their home countries, investments in their fullest possible integration were more often than not delayed and devalued.

Indeed, the old system creates additional dependencies by denying the right to work to asylum seekers whose claim is thought to be plausible, or to the immediate family members of immigrants with residence rights. A new system would ensure immediate access to labour markets, which would also reduce immigrants' needs to draw upon social assistance resources.

Finally, the old thinking considers sending-country governments either as big parts of the migration problem or as agents for receiving repatriated migrants. Neither the migrants nor their home countries are considered genuine partners in development or in mobility management.

Since the old system is mired in thinking that has led to the European Union's policy and political quagmire on migration, the new system needs to devise a more positive discourse and, more importantly, holistic positions that are more responsive to the realities of international migration. For this to occur, progress must be made in several areas.

The new system should not be thought of as an immigration system at all: instead, it should be conceptualised as an emerging system of international labour mobility. Those that govern the new mobility system should be willing to shape it. Specifically, they need to:

—   make clear to migrants what is expected of them and what they can expect;

—   be willing to explain the logic and rationale of immigration policies to the electorate and defend the new system against its detractors;

—   engage with migrants and their countries of origin as genuine partners in governing the mobility system; and

—   be willing to adjust immigration postures to reflect both changing circumstances and the results from ongoing evaluations.

ISBN: 978-92-64-03740-3 © OECD 2007

Rather than thinking exclusively in terms of regional (EU), national, or sub-national talent pools, governments of the new system must demonstrate that they can understand and take advantage of global, regional (i.e. other than EU), inter-regional and sub-regional mobility systems. Moreover, the conception of immigration as a problem seeking solution must give way to a conception of labour flows as a means for solving economic problems in source and receiving countries, calling for coherent policies in the framework of an overall development strategy.

Governments, under the new system, cannot remain captive to the now unproductive debate about whether or not to open immigration to skilled or unskilled workers (the era of rhetorical goals of zero immigration is now past). They must forge policy conversations with all relevant stakeholders (e.g. employer associations, unions, migrants' organisations and local governments) about the workers needed in the economy and that the society is prepared to accept, treat properly and integrate effectively.

In the new system, governments can no longer be held up by abstract or ideological debates about permanent or temporary workers. They need to recruit workers that fill real needs, regardless of their ultimate immigration status. Only then can visas be allocated based on the characteristics of the job in question, its expected duration, and the qualifications of its prospective occupant. Governments need to ensure that investments in assimilating migrants economically and politically, and in accepting them socially, are integral policies of the new system. Accordingly, within the new system, governments will make most permanent immigration decisions sometime after admission, thus using the early stages of work visas as probationary periods. Temporary workers who demonstrate their ability to remain in the labour market, to abide by all rules, to learn the national language at functional levels and to meet other reasonable requirements can graduate into permanent status. In this scheme, temporary foreign-worker visas would become formally what they often are in practice today for those who choose to see them as such — transitional or provisional permanent immigration visas.

It may be advantageous for governments in the new system to experiment with new visa types (multi-year, multi-entry, multi-activity) and different forms of migration. Circular migration can be one such form[2]. Unlike earlier temporary or rotational work-visa schemes, the new visa policies should not be based on debates about whether the visa holder may wish to stay or go back, but be devised upon a spectrum of incentives and disincentives to allow circularity and accomplish policy goals.

ISBN: 978-92-64-03740-3 © OECD 2007

Proper wages and benefits, labour rights, work-related health protection and short-term unemployment insurance should be available to all and remain receiving-state responsibilities. Governments in the new mobility system, however, could also experiment with new forms of internationally portable social-welfare benefits. These additional forms of social protection could be provided based on a system of graduated rights and responsibilities. Until the attainment of full citizenship, the corresponding responsibility for migrants would dictate that they (and their sponsors) pay for access to additional state-funded training or education programmes, all but catastrophic health-care coverage and longer-term social insurance, via new instruments, such as bonds and transitional social-insurance systems, which could be underwritten. Although the present social dimension of the European Union would likely not allow this kind of differentiation between native and migrant workers, many of the efficiencies of this graduated rights and responsibilities scheme could nevertheless be realised if there were substantially greater portability of social protection rights and benefits. Portability of this kind will require reforms that are difficult (each social security system is different) but not impossible[3].

Immigration policies of the new system must be implemented alongside fundamental reforms in educational and training regimes, radical changes to government labour market regulation, and social and health insurance reforms in order to create competitive economies that serve national interests well in a global economy. The feasibility of such radical changes varies from country to country, but the costs of inaction are great in all EU member states. In all cases, partisans of reforms will find their task easier to the extent that they can demonstrate benefits for many parties: native workers, migrants, employers, and states in receiving and sending countries.

The Age of Mobility

The current era might well come to be known as the "age of mobility". More people will move more frequently, prompted not only by gaps in living standards and advances in transportation and communications, but also by two other major factors: the global competition for talent and the new demographics, which juxtaposes the developed world's fast-growing old-age bulge with the developing world's rapidly growing youth bulge. (Migration trends are summarised in Box 2.2. and the current foreign-born populations in the EU27 countries are presented in Table 2.2.)

ISBN: 978-92-64-03740-3 © OECD 2007

Box 2.2. Migration Trends: The European Experience

There are currently about 40 million expatriates (foreign-born individuals) in the EU27 countries, representing about 8.3 per cent of their total population. Of the foreign-born adults living in the EU25, 74 per cent are low- or medium-skilled and only 26 per cent are highly skilled (Münz *et al.*, 2006a). Overall, Europe lags behind North America in attracting highly skilled migrants (Katseli *et al.*, 2006a). According to available data which pertain only to the EU15, the EU15 countries have attracted only one-quarter of the total number of highly skilled migrants. In contrast, two-thirds of all such migrants are found in North America. More than half of the foreign-born migrants in the EU15 come from other EU15 countries. A great part of the other half (26.4 per cent) come from the wider Europe area and North Africa. Migration of low-skilled workers to the EU originates primarily from neighbouring countries[*]. High-skilled workers to the EU are drawn from further afield, including Africa[**].

Migration patterns vary across EU member states. In fact, there is considerable heterogeneity across different EU countries, both in terms of immigrant characteristics as well as countries of origin. As one might expect, there is a North/South divide in Europe. More than 50 per cent of the foreign-born population in the most industrialised EU countries (France, the United Kingdom, Ireland, Belgium, the Netherlands, Finland, Sweden, Denmark and Luxembourg) came from other EU15 or OECD countries. By contrast, this share is considerably lower in southern Europe and in Germany; in these countries, more than 50 per cent of the foreign-born population originated in transition or developing economies.

The 2007 OECD *International Migration Outlook* report indicates that immigration has risen sharply in certain European countries, most notably in Spain, Italy and the United Kingdom (the largest proportional increases in the European Union members of the OECD were witnessed in Austria, the United Kingdom and Sweden); it has declined in others, including Germany, France and Portugal. The number of asylum seekers has steadily declined, while the number of foreign students has increased (the largest proportional increases observed in Czech Republic, the southern European countries, Ireland, France and the Netherlands, some starting from low levels). The list of leading countries of origin for migrants to Europe has seen some important reshuffling in recent years — even if many of the quickly rising countries have been important sources of emigration for many years. Thus, the relative importance of European immigration from Ukraine, China, the Russian Federation and countries in Latin America has risen dramatically. In 2000, immigrant flows to Europe were mostly from Morocco, Ecuador, Poland, Bulgaria, Turkey and Romania[***]. By 2005, the order of importance of the main sending countries has changed: Poland, Romania, Morocco and Bulgaria. The 2007 *International Migration Outlook* also reveals that, while Latin American countries used to send few migrants to Europe, since 2000, 150 000-200 000 immigrants arrive annually in Europe from that region, going mostly to Spain.

Notes:

* EU15 residents from wider Europe and North Africa accounted for 35 per cent of the total stock of low-skilled foreign born (OECD Database on Foreign-born and Expatriates).

** High-skilled Africans comprised 13.5 per cent of the highly skilled EU15 residents born in non-OECD countries (OECD Database on Foreign-born and Expatriates).

*** Apart from these countries, there are also some OECD member countries that send large numbers of migrants to other OECD (and European) countries, including Germany, the UK, the USA, France and Italy.

Table 2.2 Foreign Nationals and Foreign-born Population in EU27 (latest available year)

	Foreign Nationals[a]						Foreign Born[a]					
	Total		Citizen of another EU27 country		Citizen of a country outside the EU27		Total		Born in another EU27 country		Born in a country outside the EU27	
	thousands	% of population	thousands	% of population	thousands	% of population	thousands	% of population	thousands	% of population	thousands	% of population
EU27	22 888	4.7	8 462[b]	1.7[b]	14 426[b]	2.9[b]	40 501	8.3	13 222[c]	2.7[c]	27 279[c]	5.6[c]
Austria	777	9.5	272	3.3	505	6.2	1 234	15.1	489	6.0	745	9.1
Belgium	871	8.4	618	6.0	253	2.4	1 186	11.4	611	5.9	575	5.5
Bulgaria	26	0.3					104	1.3				
Cyprus[d]	65	9.4	35	5.1	30	4.3	116	13.9	44	5.3	72	8.6
Czech Republic	254	2.5	126	1.2	128	1.3	453	4.4	344	3.3	109	1.1
Denmark	268	4.9	91	1.7	177	3.2	389	7.2	116	2.2	273	5.0
Estonia	95	6.9	(3)	(0.2)	92	6.7	202	15.2	(10)	(0.8)	192	14.4
Finland	108	2.1	46	0.9	62	1.2	156	3.0	63	1.2	93	1.8
France	3 263	5.6	1 278	2.2	1 985	3.4	6 471	10.7	2 125	3.5	4 346	7.2
Germany	6 739	8.9	2 385	3.1	4 354	5.8	10 144	12.3				
Greece	762	7.0	163	1.5	599	5.5	974	8.8	214	1.9	760	6.9
Hungary	142	1.4	92	0.9	50	0.5	316	3.1	200	2.0	116	1.1
Ireland	223	5.5	152	3.7	71	1.8	585	14.1	429	10.3	156	3.8
Italy	2 402	4.1					2 519	4.3				
Latvia	103	3.9	(10)	(0.4)	93	3.5	449	19.5	43	1.9	406	17.6
Lithuania	21	0.6	(5)	(0.1)	16	0.5	165	4.8	11	0.3	154	4.5
Luxembourg	177	39.0					174	37.4				
Malta	13	3.2	6	1.5	7	1.7	11	2.7	4	1.0	7	1.7
Netherlands	699	4.3	261	1.6	438	2.7	1 736	10.6	354	2.2	1 382	8.4
Poland	49	0.1	(12)	(0.03)	37	0.1	703	1.8	241	0.6	462	1.2
Portugal	449	4.3	90	0.9	359	3.4	764	7.3	178	1.7	586	5.6
Romania	26	0.1					103	0.6				
Slovakia	22	0.4	(12)	(0.2)	(10)	(0.2)	124	2.3	106	2.0	18	0.3
Slovenia	37	1.9	(4)	(0.2)	(33)	(1.7)	167	8.5	14	0.7	153	7.8
Spain	1 977	4.6	594	1.4	1 383	3.2	4 790	11.1	1 405	3.3	3 385	7.8
Sweden	463	5.1	205	2.3	258	2.8	1 117	12.4	558	6.2	559	6.2
United Kingdom	2 857	2.9	1 131	1.1	1 726	1.8	5 408	9.1	1 592	2.7	3 816	6.4

Notes:

a) Data on the total foreign-national and foreign-born populations are from OECD (2006), UN (2006) and national statistics. The totals are split between "other EU27" and "outside EU27" on the basis of estimations computed with data from the European Labour Force Survey (2005).

b) For the estimation of the EU27 total, we assume that the foreign nationals in Bulgaria, Italy, Luxembourg and Romania (for which there are no data available in the LFS) are distributed among "other EU27" and "outside EU27" in the same way as the average of the remaining EU27 countries.

c) For the estimation of the EU27 total, we assume that the foreign-born in Bulgaria, Germany, Italy, Luxembourg and Romania (for which there are no data available in the LFS) are distributed among "other EU27" and "outside EU27" in the same way as the average of the remaining EU27 countries.

d) Greek part of Cyprus only.

Data in brackets are of limited reliability because of the small sample size.

Source: OECD (2006), UN (2006), European Labour Force Survey (LFS) ad hoc modules (2005), and national statistics. This table has been published in Münz et al. (2006b).

ISBN: 978-92-64-03740-3 © OECD 2007

The age of mobility may also mean that the composition of migrants by gender will change over time. Until the mid-1970s, there was little research on female migration. Only from the 1980s onwards did it become clear that woman migrate in large numbers — through family reunification, but also as independent migrants. Moreover, it is increasingly clear that migration affects women differently from men. Some argue that migration leads to more independence for women who earn their own money, send remittances and make autonomous decisions. Others point out that the skills of female migrants working abroad in service occupations might result in significant deskilling.

Table 2.3 shows, for a selection of EU member states and some other OECD countries, the percentage of women in the foreign-born population between 1993 and 2003. The table similarly shows the proportion of foreign-born women for 1993, 1996, 2001 and 2003 in Australia, Canada, New Zealand and the United States. The figures show a rise in the female share of the foreign population over the decade in many, but not all, countries; moreover, in several countries women comprise more than half of the foreign population. Further details on foreign-born women in the European labour force are presented in Box 2.3.

Table 2.3 **Women as a Share of the Foreign or Foreign-born Population, Selected OECD Countries**

	Share of Foreign Women in the Total Foreign Population			
	1993	1997	2000	2003
Japan	..	..	..	53.8
United Kingdom	54.4	53.5	53.1	52.0
Hungary	..	..	50.9	51.5
Denmark	..	..	50.6	50.9
Norway	48.1	51.3	50.5	50.7
Finland	..	48.1	50.5	50.5
Sweden	49.8	50.6	50.9	50.4
Netherlands	45.8	47.3	48.4	49.3
Belgium	..	47.6	48.3	48.6
Switzerland	44.9	46.2	47.0	47.0
Germany	33.4	34.9	45.7	46.9
Spain	..	..	45.4	44.9
Korea	..	39.0	41.9	40.9
Portugal	..	41.7	42.8	36.6

	Share of Immigrant Women in the Foreign-born Population			
	1993	1996	2001	2003
Australia	48.9	..	..	50.3
Canada	..	51.6	51.9	..
United States	..	51.0	50.3	49.9
New Zealand	..	..	51.5	..

Source: OECD (2005).

ISBN: 978-92-64-03740-3 © OECD 2007

Box 2.3. **Foreign-born Women in the European Labour Force**

How many migrant women are in the labour force? Table 2.4 provides some information regarding this question, presenting the share of women among foreign or foreign-born labour force participants for several European Union member states and a handful of other OECD countries. (The labour force includes all those working-age people who hold a job or are actively seeking work.) Like the female share of the foreign or foreign-born, the share of women among migrant workers has risen over the period represented here in virtually all countries. In no country, however, are women more than half of working migrants. Additionally, the share of women in the foreign or foreign-born labour force is less than that of women (of all nationalities) in the labour force, except in Canada and the United Kingdom.

Much of the growth in the employment rates of immigrant women over the last decade (particularly in southern Europe) was oriented towards low-skilled occupations such as domestic services, health care, and social services, as well as tourism and catering services and, to a lesser extent, education. This is due in part to the growing demand for domestic services (including child care) following the increasing participation of native women in the labour force. It is also a result of the growing need for assistance to the elderly due to the ageing populations in most OECD countries.

Female immigrants face specific difficulties in integrating into the labour market in many destination countries, as they face many types of discrimination, based on language barriers, their citizenship/ethnicity or their own child-care needs. Even if on the whole the employment rates of female immigrants have grown over the past decade in parallel to those of the native born, female immigrants still participate disproportionately less in the labour market than their male counterparts and native-born females. Quantitative analysis reveals that even controlling for levels of education and age, immigrant women's employment has tended to decline relative to that of native-born women in several countries (Austria, Germany, the Netherlands and the United Kingdom). Only in Sweden and France do immigrant women's employment rates seem to have grown more rapidly than those of the native born.

Improving migrant women's labour-market participation boosts social equity but also short and long-term economic efficiency[4].

ISBN: 978-92-64-03740-3 © OECD 2007

Table 2.4. **Women as a Share of the Foreign or Foreign-born Labour Force**

	Share of Foreign Female Workers in the Foreign Labour Force				Percentage of Women in the Total Labour Force
	1993	1997	2001	2003	2003
Austria	33.5	33.6	36.3	36.8	44.6
Belgium	..	33.6	34.7	34.9	43.1
Korea	..	29.0	302.0	29.4	41.0
Denmark	42.3	42.6	43.6	44.1	46.4
Spain	29.9	34.6	34.3	35.5	40.5
France	34.2	35.7	38.4	39.3	46.0
Greece	..	..	40.9	..	40.0
Italy	30.8	31.4	30.3	..	39.1
Netherlands	..	..	..	41.3	44.1
Sweden	45.7	45.9	47.1	46.6	47.7
Switzerland	34.7	36.8	38.0	39.9	45.2
United Kingdom	49.0	..	44.3	45.6	45.8
	Share of Immigrant Women Workers in the Foreign-born Labour Force				
	1993	1997	2001	2003	2003
Australia	40.1	..	..	46.3	44.7
Canada	44.4	..	46.3	46.5	46.5
United States	..	41.2	41.3	41.2	46.6
New Zealand	..	..	46.2	..	46.0

Source: OECD (2005).

The new mobility system will also require a new set of relationships between public and non-governmental sectors, including the private sector. Social partners and broader civil society, including diaspora networks, must become co-architects of and share responsibility for the implementation of the system, or there is real risk it will be unstable and ineffective. To get the maximum value from the new mobility system, market forces and civil society must be converted into partners. Working against, rather than with, market forces is an exercise in futility. Working with the active engagement of civil society — the main stakeholders — legitimises decision-making processes and increases knowledge about the needs and rights of the stakeholders. A co-operative approach to designing the new system also means that all sides can share responsibilities.

In the emerging mobility age, opportunities and challenges alike will arise throughout society, requiring a "whole-of-society" approach to moving ahead. This is no less ambitious than revising the social compact. And it will certainly require a "whole-of-government" approach to decision making.

ISBN: 978-92-64-03740-3 © OECD 2007

Single-purpose policies, just as single-cause explanations, are poor guides in developing successful responses to intricate and politically sensitive issues. Although government competencies are almost always focused on single issues and bureaucracies are typically organised vertically in order to deliver the necessary function, decisions that relate to migration cut across policy domains and administrative responsibilities and thus require extraordinary co-ordination in both planning and execution.

Examples abound of the need for, and benefits of, more coherent and horizontally co-ordinated policy making. Effective immigration control policies require that foreign policy, development co-operation policies, labour-market regulation (and deregulation), education and workforce development, and interior and workplace standards enforcement, among others, work in concert to deliver desired outcomes.

A new system theref+ore needs inter-ministerial co-ordination at the level of EU member states, which also must be matched within the Commission apparatus as well: a range of directorates-general (DG) (most notably DG Justice, Freedom and Security; DG Employment, Social Affairs and Equal Opportunities, and DG Development) must work together to address migration policy. Similarly the working party configuration — inter-ministerial communication mechanisms of varying degrees of formality — must be used and strengthened where applicable (Katseli *et al.*, 2006a). (Since October 2006, it is important to note, there is a Commissioners' Group on Migration involving several of the directorates- general mentioned above, in addition to Economic and Financial Affairs, Health, Regional Policy, Education and Culture, Internal Market and Trade.)

These national and regional efforts towards greater policy coherence will require increased international co-ordination as well, between the EU, its member states, and migrants' home countries.

For immigrant selection systems to work well, for example, educational and training organisations, together with enterprises and business associations, must identify areas of skill shortages and mismatches at the earliest possible time and devise ways to address them effectively. In the area of education and training, greater regional, international and global qualification frameworks are needed to address more effectively the problem of mutual recognition of qualifications.

ISBN: 978-92-64-03740-3 © OECD 2007

Prerequisites for and Challenges to the New Mobility System

In crafting a new mobility system, governments face three principal challenges: how to foster public confidence in governments' capacity to manage migration in order to generate support for the new policies and institutions; how to allocate tasks across levels of government — local, national, regional and global; and how to ensure migrants' integration into host societies.

Recapturing Control of How the Public Perceives the Migration Process

Reducing irregular and illegal migration is critical not only to protect the rights of migrants in precarious circumstances but to reassure constituents that their governments can manage migration flows. Illegal immigration is an emotive issue. The public debate surrounding it is not always sufficiently dispassionate to advise impartial policies. Sensationalist media accounts of abuses by smugglers and traffickers cannot help engender public confidence. Governments must undertake a sustained public-education effort, a task they will find easier if they move away from a rhetoric focused on keeping immigrants out towards one that underscores the benefits of immigration policies that directly address key economic and societal priorities.

Levels of Governance: Who does What?

The responsibility for management of a new mobility system must be shared among different levels of governance: sub-national governments (e.g. municipalities and regions); national governments in unilateral or bilateral arrangements; regional groupings (including supranational actors such as the European Union or the African Union); and global organisations (such as the World Trade Organization).

Where should responsibility for managing migration flows be vested? The answer depends upon the incentives faced by governments in each kind of arrangement. A case can be made for relying on a combination of such levels of governance. The precise combination, however, will differ according to the geopolitical setting and local circumstances.

When is a supranational process — such as management by the European Commission — better than a unilateral or bilateral arrangement? A national government will be willing to move away from unilateral decisions on migration if it has a direct hand in setting the rules of the process or if it can exert significant influence on the process as it is managed day to day. Additionally, a country might also be pushed to enter a supranational decision-making process if the transaction costs of reaching domestic consensus on international migration become too high. In that case, a government benefits because the supranational process restricts its domestic bargaining space (tying its hands), thereby facilitating internal implementation of the policy in question. Such conditions are especially salient where immigration flows are large and accelerating (as is the case in Ireland, Spain and the United Kingdom). Alternatively, if a country's leadership feels it has no hand in setting the rules or monitoring the implementation of a regional or multilateral initiative, or if transaction costs are relatively low, it is likely to prefer unilateral or bilateral action on migration management.

Regional processes[5], even when they offer greater opportunities for all participants, are costly to manage: adjustments are more difficult to make and monitoring and enforcement of non-compliance are typically far more complicated in regional settings than in bilateral ones. Regional processes thus require institutional and intergovernmental mechanisms to reach binding agreements and, more importantly, the power to enforce compliance meaningfully, including with countries of unauthorised migrant origin and transit. Once reached, however, regional agreements are more difficult to renegotiate or bypass, ensuring a greater degree of compliance and more effective implementation.

Thus, a shift from unilateralism/bilateralism to regionalism and multilateralism is likely to take place when the benefits of collective action increase, and when the costs of migration policy making — including the costs of domestic consensus building — increase sufficiently to offset the costs of regional or multilateral institution building. Such a shift in preferences can be observed in Europe today, even if multilateral initiatives are still quite new. Ten to 15 years ago, bilateral initiatives prevailed. For example, Italy addressed the rapid influx of Albanian immigration by working bilaterally with Albania, which made eminent sense. Similarly, in the early 1990s, Germany created a special agricultural-worker scheme for Polish workers (spurred in part by uncertainties about the magnitude of uncontrolled flows in the wake of the collapse of the Communist system) to manage better the two countries' migration relationship. Germany reinforced this move later in the decade by pushing successfully for accession of Poland (and much of that region) to the EU. Today, however, more and more European countries face increasing opposition to large immigration flows and are seeking to co-ordinate, if not to harmonise, their policies in the context of a European process.

The European Commission increasingly feels the pressure to assume leadership in migration management by issuing directives that would

ISBN: 978-92-64-03740-3 © OECD 2007

harmonise practices across member states or introduce new, more flexible mobility arrangements (the 2007 communication on mobility partnerships is a noteworthy example: European Commission 2007b). But it will remain on the sidelines of migration management until it is explicitly granted authority to do so. The Commission needs the authority to monitor migration flows, to strengthen internal and intergovernmental co-ordination mechanisms, and to negotiate migration accords with sending countries that include work visas and other concessions. Until member states permit the European Commission to enter into and enforce such agreements, its authority in the emerging mobility system will be strictly secondary.

Many will find this judgment too severe, particularly in light of the migration-related competencies the EU already has: its common visa regime, for example, and the Commission's authority to negotiate many sensitive matters. But the ability to manage migration flows more effectively will increasingly hinge on the Commission's having the negotiating inducement of offering various kinds of work visas to third country nationals in return for co-operation with the Union's objectives. (The aforementioned Commission communication on Mobility Partnerships promises to take the first step towards giving the Commission this authority.)

Addressing Integration Challenges

As mobility gradually becomes the norm, integration efforts will have to intensify accordingly. As relationships between host societies and immigrants evolve, an emphasis on mutuality, on creating common space and on developing an inclusive community identity can help a society move forward. Collaborative integration efforts that engage the government, the private sector and civil society can help immigrants become, and be seen as, long-term contributors to the community. Ultimately, integration efforts succeed best when they reconcile the immigrants' needs and interests with those of the broader community in a dynamic process that weaves a new social fabric.

Sub-national and local levels of government also have critical roles in addressing the challenges of integration. By its very nature, integration will always be first and foremost a local affair. The critical interaction between newcomers and the larger community occur at the local level. It is here where success and failure — and hence effective policy innovation — happen most naturally. Of course, national governments typically provide the resources for integration, and also create the enabling legal environment within which policy or programme experiments occur and performance is measured. Managing integration in a durable fashion has to be a bottom-up process, building on the

ISBN: 978-92-64-03740-3 © OECD 2007

experience of local communities, rather than a top-down process to be diffused to the lower levels. An EU integration strategy would therefore be a combination of member states' experiences and practices, allowing considerable margins of flexibility to suit the particular circumstances of any given member state in managing integration.

In sum, it is often the case that the European Commission has been sidelined by its member states' efforts on the management of flows on the one hand, and by sub-national governments' efforts in integration, on the other. These realities should not lead the reader to underestimate the Commission's role, which is likely to grow in importance. Its effectiveness will fluctuate with the maturing of decision making in the Commission and the thoughtfulness and quality of its interventions.

The quality of the Commission's interventions, in turn, will be influenced greatly by seven interrelated factors:

— the Commission's commitment to monitoring admission and integration practices as well as outcomes in member states;

— the Commission's ability to issue new directives that expand the options for legal migration and provide flexible arrangements for staying and working in the European Union;

— the Commission's courage to act when member states fail to make sufficient progress on integration (i.e. demonstrating its willingness to deal effectively with the perennial issues of legal competence and deference to member state sensitivities);

— the quality of civil society engagement with the European Commission;

— the resources available to seed new initiatives and fund corrective region-wide policies;

— the degree to which migration policy is rendered more coherent with other relevant policy domains, notably trade, development and the social dimensions of globalisation; and

— the Commission's ability to enter into mobility partnerships with sending countries to improve the management of flows and share more fairly the benefits and burdens of increased mobility.

Whether or not the age of mobility is already upon us or just over the horizon, the only projection one can make is that mobility in all its forms will increase. This reality demands that understanding mobility is a prerequisite both to shaping it and to managing it better.

ISBN: 978-92-64-03740-3 © OECD 2007

Notes

1. See Papademetriou and Yale-Loehr, 1996; Meissner *et al.*, 2006; we return to this aspect of family-based migration in the section of Chapter 3 entitled *Opportunities for Permanent Residence and Citizenship*.

2. Circular migration is identified with repetitive migration, whether seasonal or temporary. Seasonal employment refers to stays of less than a year's duration; all other types of agreement with stays exceeding one year are referred to as temporary. Both seasonal and temporary migration can be repetitive if the same individual crosses borders more than once over time.

3. International best practices for portability of social protection rights and benefits are analysed in Holzmann *et al.* (2005).

4. For more information on migrant women and the labour market, see the series of papers written for a joint EC-OECD seminar on "Migrant women and the labour market: diversity and challenges", Brussels, 26-27 September 2005. The papers can be accessed from the following site: http://ec.europa.eu/employment_social/employment_analysis/imm_migr_wom05_en.htm

5. The regional processes referred to here are typically regional "dialogues" co-ordinated by the International Organization for Migration.

Chapter 3

Migration and Employment: Labour Market Access Policies

As acknowledged previously, it is likely that the demand for both highly and low- or semi- skilled immigrants will continue to increase. These different types of migration call for a range of policies governing access to labour markets.

Finding and retaining the workers, particularly skilled workers — in terms of both vocational and educational skills — that EU member states' economies will need in the coming years will become increasingly difficult. For the near-term, the overwhelming majority of these workers will come from within the Union. The demographic reality of an ageing population in virtually all EU countries, however, means a significant and constantly increasing number will have to be drawn from non-member sending countries. Moreover, finding skilled foreign workers is already challenging given the stiffening global competition for talent, particularly in such fields as health care, the sciences and information and communications technology (ICT) — and this challenge will only become more acute (Münz *et al.*, 2006*a*, 2006*b*; Katseli *et al.*, 2006*a*; and Katseli *et al.*, 2006*b*).

Many EU member states are already experiencing labour-market shortages in selected sectors (Münz *et al.*, 2006*a*, and 2006*b*). Among the economic sectors that are already suffering are ICT, financial services, household services, agricultural, transportation, construction and tourism-related services, such as the hotel and restaurant industries. The unfriendly environments that many immigrants face in various European countries further complicate the challenge. Rather than viewing immigration as a force to be harnessed for greatest mutual benefit, many states have instead seen immigration as a threat to be countered and even overcome.

The age of mobility demands the creation of a mobility system transparent to all users, responsive to the needs of employers, and mindful of the importance of creating welcoming environments. Creating such a system poses a special challenge for the European Union. While the Union's market for goods and services is moving towards seamlessness, its labour market remains fragmented. Specifically, workers from EU member states who joined after 2004 cannot work throughout the Union, and legally resident third-country nationals across the Union generally are unable to deploy their skills outside their state of residence. This fragmentation further undermines the appeal of the EU to skilled immigrants, who have the option of working in the much more receptive environments in North America, Oceania and increasingly in Asia. Clearly, EU and member state policy makers will have to strive for trans-Union cohesiveness as they reinvent their mobility systems.

In recent years the European Union and its member states have taken some stage-setting steps towards establishing a legal framework for managing immigration flows. The political mandate for doing so can be traced back to the European Council at Tampere in October 1999, the conclusions of which called for "more efficient management of migration flows at all their stages" and provided for a common migration policy that included legal migration and integration (European Council, 1999). Building upon the political foundation laid at Tampere, the European Council of November 2004 approved the Hague Programme, which calls for a "comprehensive approach, involving all stages of migration, with respect to the root causes of migration, entry and admission policies and integration and return policies" (European Council, 2004*a*).

While European policy making in the area of migration management is relatively recent, several initiatives have been adopted. These concern various groups of foreigners: the status of third-country nationals who are long-term residents, as well as family re-unification (European Council, 2003); the admission of researchers (European Council, 2005) and of students (European Council, 2004*b*) from third countries. The European Commission's Policy Plan on Legal Migration (European Commission, 2005*a*), proposed four directives for the management of entry and residence of highly skilled workers, seasonal workers, intra-corporate transferees and remunerated trainees respectively. With its communication on "A Common Agenda for Integration" (European Commission, 2005*b*), the Commission also put forward a framework for the integration of third-country nationals in the EU. Another recent Commission communication, "Migration and Development", highlights the importance of enhancing collaboration with migrant-sending countries on economic migration and of developing initiatives offering advantageous opportunities to countries

ISBN: 978-92-64-03740-3 © OECD 2007

of origin and destination and to labour migrants (European Commission, 2005c). It suggests a number of initiatives in the realms of remittances, collaboration with diasporas, circular migration and mitigation of the adverse effect of the brain drain.

The Hague Programme agenda (European Council, 2004a) is a start to addressing the failures of earlier attempts to regulate immigration flows into the EU and facilitate the integration of immigrants into labour markets and society. Arguably, the main weaknesses of the earlier policies were regulations that were both too many and too specific, and they did not adequately take into account market realities and participants' incentives.

As earlier noted, shortages of skills and geographic mismatches across EU labour markets are projected to increase over the next two decades. Immigration, of both high- and low-skilled workers, to fill labour needs will increase. These flows have to be managed sensitively to address the needs for transparency, responsiveness and cohesiveness. Accordingly policy innovation could be pursued in several areas. We recommend that:

— the EU and its member states must develop an Integrated Migration Monitoring System to provide effective monitoring of flows;

— labour-market access policies should be adopted that abet circular migration for those workers in critical occupational categories who do not aim for (or who will not be likely to be granted) permanent residence;

— cross-EU harmonisation must provide uniform access to all member-state labour markets for defined categories of skilled workers; and

— labour-market access and citizenship policies must be attractive to those workers — highly skilled or not — needed by EU member states and who seek eventually the security and stability of permanent residence and citizenship.

Given that demand for low-skilled and semi-skilled migration will continue to increase in the decades ahead, we further recommend that the EU may want to engage in an informal but inclusive policy dialogue among all relevant stakeholders on GATS Mode 4 provision (See Box 3.1).

Decisive action in these areas — discussed in greater detail in the remainder of this chapter — will increase the likelihood that EU member states will be better able to attract workers they will need. However, attracting them (and, more importantly, retaining them when appropriate) will require policy advances in the realm of integration; these are addressed in Chapter 4 of this report.

ISBN: 978-92-64-03740-3 © OECD 2007

Box 3.1 **GATS Mode 4: Better Organised Mobility of Service Providers?**

The European Union is not the only supra-national political organisation that can regulate labour mobility in Europe. Under the General Agreement on Trade in Services (GATS), part of the World Trade Organization (WTO) treaty, services can be provided by suppliers in one country to consumers in another through the Mode 4 supply, namely the movement of natural persons to the country of the consumer. Mode 4 movements for service provision encompass temporary movements which involve self-employed persons based in the country of origin and/or employees of a contract service provider also based in the country of origin. Given that unfilled labour-market gaps will only increase in European countries in the future, and given this report's emphasis on providing more (and more flexible) channels for entry of workers for varying durations, it is reasonable to ask whether an expansion of GATS Mode 4 movements could respond to this need.

Under the conditions of the GATS, WTO member countries negotiate access for service providers in certain sectors of the economy. To date, Mode 4 movements have been dominated by transfers of relatively high-level executives within a company. This kind of movement tends to accompany foreign direct investment; a foreign firm buys a domestic firm and then transfers managers to the new location. The text of the GATS is not limited to such intra-corporate transfers, however, and some experts have suggested extending Mode 4 negotiations to a wider range of service providers, particularly those with low- and middle-range skill levels (UNCTAD, 2003; Winters *et al.*, 2003).

Mode 4 negotiations promise more effective management of service provision by directly implicating foreign firms — providers and demanders of services — and by extending the set of options for labour mobility. Movement of workers under Mode 4 implies a sharing of risks that is different from other kinds of mobility: in the presence of foreign intermediaries, the ultimate responsibility for ensuring both the return of workers to the country of origin and/or the continued employment of the imported worker can be credibly borne by the foreign employer, the country of origin, or a combination of employers from the host and home countries. Working arrangements can specify appropriate remuneration, length of stay and working conditions*. Negotiating countries and firms can design appropriate insurance schemes. Mode 4 movements for lower-skilled service providers are controversial in developed countries — witness the acrimonious accusations of "social dumping" surrounding the failed Bolkestein directive in 2005 (European Commission (2004)), which sought essentially similar regulations for cross-border service provision in the European Union. Nevertheless, taking Mode 4 negotiations in this direction would be of great interest to low- and middle-income countries where many such service providers are located; putting Mode 4 on the agenda would furthermore increase the interest of developing countries in reaching a

ISBN: 978-92-64-03740-3 © OECD 2007

Box 3.1 (contd.)

successful resolution to the current Doha round of WTO negotiations. For all these reasons, and because of the promise of a better organised market for service provision, European countries (and others) may wish to promote an informal and inclusive policy dialogue on GATS Mode 4 provision.

Note: * With regard to the European Commission's directive 96/71/EC on posting of workers, and COM(2006)458 on the implementation of the directive, undertakings established in a non-member state must not be given more favourable treatment than undertakings established in a member state. The European Union, in this vein, has expressed a commitment to ensure that EU trade policy (including policy related to trade in services) is consistent with the internal EU framework for services of general interest.

An Integrated Migration-Monitoring System

For more effective labour-market policy making, information on migration flows needs to be substantially improved through better collection of data, statistical capacity building, and more effective harmonisation and data sharing across countries. The European Commission's Policy Plan on Legal Migration proposes some useful first steps, most notably that information contained in the European Job Mobility Portal (EURES) and the network created to foster mobility of EU nationals be expanded to support the management of economic immigration of third-country nationals and provide information on incoming as well as returning migrants (European Commission, 2005a). Moreover, the new European Migration Network and the forthcoming Migration Statistics regulations are part of the Commission's efforts towards obtaining more and better data on migration. But more is needed. One such measure, an *Integrated Migration-Monitoring System* to collect and process relevant information based on data and metadata by member countries would provide a useful resource for migration flows. Using a unique identification number provided to all non-EU nationals legally entering the community, such a system could provide effective and evidence-based monitoring of inflows and outflows as well as the necessary information that could guide policy making.

Temporary and Circular Migration

For many migrants, grants of permanent residency and citizenship (the reform of which is discussed in the section of Chapter 3 entitled *Effective Free Movement within the European Union*) might not be a necessary precondition of entry. As a general rule, the lower the skill requirements of a job the less likely it is that receiving societies will be willing to grant the job holder permanent residence.

ISBN: 978-92-64-03740-3 © OECD 2007

Recent years have seen a proliferation of temporary employment schemes offering a variety of pre-admission and post-admission incentives and disincentives designed to keep flows temporary. The International Labour Organization reports a plethora of temporary schemes in use by different OECD and developing countries (Abella, 2006). In many EU countries, such agreements have always served as an alternative to long-term work contracts and permanent residence.

In order to be effective, new schemes will need to provide adequate incentives to both employers and employees to respect them. For this reason they need to go beyond traditional guest-worker programmes that stipulated a fixed duration of stay, tied workers to a specific employer and tried to force their rotation. Such schemes often introduced programmatic and labour market distortions and made the management of the flows more difficult over time: businesses initiated (or deferred) investments on the presumption of a continuous supply of immigrant labour while migrants had little opportunity (or incentive) to change jobs or an incentive to leave the country (Martin, 2006).

Effective management of successful temporary programmes needs to be associated, instead, with flexible working arrangements and involve consultation with all stakeholders, close supervision of recruitment procedures, clear admission criteria, and steadfast protection of all labour and associated social rights. They must also address the fact that under present arrangements, uncertain prospects for re-entry to the EU discourage migrants from returning home. Not the least among governments' concerns will be how to garner and maintain public support for temporary migration initiatives (Rannveig Agunias and Newland, 2007). As such, we recommend four specific policies to encourage temporary or circular migration.

- Issue multi-use, multi-annual work permits

In rethinking temporary schemes, circular migration arrangements associated with multi-entry, multi-annual visas for short-term work under flexible contracts for service provision should be developed. Seasonal migration of Polish workers to Germany has over the past years provided a good example of circular migration (See Box 3.2). Indeed, temporary visa programmes allowing workers to work and train for a limited period in EU countries could fill gaps in EU countries (e.g. in the health-care system) while encouraging skill circulation that mitigates some of the more damaging consequences of the brain drain to migrant-sending countries. There is a possibility that the migrant may choose not to return

ISBN: 978-92-64-03740-3 © OECD 2007

home upon completion of the programme but instead move to a third (non-EU) country. Return home for a specified period of time could be made a prerequisite for granting a re-entry visa to an EU country in the future. Whether such programmes should be focused upon countries that currently supply significant numbers of health-care workers or teachers to EU countries, or upon those countries most in need of additional personnel in these fields, also warrants careful scrutiny.

- Lower the cost of re-entry and offer flexible procedures for re-admission of workers

To allow workers to come and go across borders in an organised fashion under contracts of fixed duration, recruitment through intermediaries and flexible procedures for admission and re-admission need to be introduced; incentives need also to be provided for contract enforcement and legal return. Workers, for example, could be admitted initially for probationary periods consistent with the nature of the work (e.g. seasonal, high-peak, training regime or project-tied). If after one or more successive assignments a worker proves capable of complying to the fixed duration of his or her contract, by returning home and re-entering legally to work, while showing aptitude in learning the national language, contracts could be prolonged and the possibility opened for future permanent residence (Papademetriou and Meissner, 2006).

Box 3.2 **Polish Seasonal Migration to Germany**

Seasonal migration of Polish workers to Germany provides a good example of circular migration: the same workers cross borders year after year to work in a neighbouring country for a short period of time, on the basis of the bilateral seasonal work permit regime (See Okólski, 2006).

Overall, Germany is the main destination for Polish migrants. The number of work permits extended by Germany to Polish workers is on the rise: in 2004, approximately 307 000 work permits were issued for seasonal work in Germany, as compared to 292 000 in 2003 and 131 000 in 1992. Recent evidence (Stark *et al.*, 2006) suggests that two-thirds of the seasonal migrants are males, many in their mid-thirties and usually married with children. In fact, 38 per cent of those who go to Germany to work as seasonal agricultural workers remain employed full-time in Poland. Their educational attainment is relatively low: about 60 per cent have not completed secondary education. They mostly come from relatively low-income regions of Poland and from medium-sized to small towns where the cost of living is substantially lower; returning to spend their income with their families in Poland allows them to increase the purchasing power of their

ISBN: 978-92-64-03740-3 © OECD 2007

Box 3.2 (contd.)

foreign earnings. Those with large families and those coming from regions with a low cost of living, in fact, tend to work longer hours than the time specified in their contracts so as to reduce the number of trips they have to undertake.

Polish seasonal workers seem to prefer circular migration to permanent relocation in Germany. Approximately 74 per cent of these workers have worked in Germany at least twice and 43 per cent at least four times. The ease of access to German labour markets for workers from new EU member states will increase considerably in 2009-2011; it will be interesting to observe whether many continue to opt for circularity under more liberal circumstances.

- Transfer pension and social security contributions to the home country

Greater portability of social security contributions (primarily pensions and, possibly, health insurance), should also be encouraged as a device to encourage circular movement. One example is the transfer of contributions to the home country, to be collected by the migrant upon return or by specified members of his or her family. In this regard, developing new institutional arrangements that can safeguard and facilitate transfers, as well as assist with the productive investment of such assets, should become a priority for the EU.

- Entitle third-country nationals enrolled in a tertiary educational institution in the EU to remain for up to two years after graduation with the purpose of seeking employment anywhere within the EU

Special consideration should be given to encouraging third-country students and graduates to work in the EU after successfully completing their studies in one of the member states. The language proficiency and social networks they have acquired will enhance their successful integration. Moreover, the (part-time) work experience they often acquire during their studies allows for a smooth transition into the labour market. Finally, the fact that they have received their education in the EU helps avoid the problem of non-recognition of qualifications that many other immigrants face. Nevertheless, the effects on their countries of origin of encouraging third-country nationals to stay must be carefully monitored. It could be that such a scheme will promote the circularity of skills; it could equally be, however, that this only accentuates the negative consequences of the brain drain.

ISBN: 978-92-64-03740-3 © OECD 2007

Training foreign students has long served as a vehicle to attract highly skilled persons from outside the EU (as is the case in North America, Oceania and elsewhere in high- and middle-income countries). During the 1990s, enrolment in EU universities of students from lower-income countries expanded rapidly. Such overseas training frequently opens important new avenues of opportunity to these students. Visas that require departure upon completion of training may not be in the best interest either of the EU member countries or of the students. Such practices may simply result, for example, in EU-trained students relocating to North America or Oceania, rather than returning to their countries of origin. Although the benefits of this training for the home country are almost certainly greater if students return home, a period of post-graduation training or work experience is a critical part of the overall learning process. For those students who wish to return home, information about opportunities there might usefully be provided systematically by university placement offices.

Effective Free Movement within the European Union

Ensuring the mobility of workers — be they EU citizens or migrants — is extremely important for responsive labour markets and efficient economies (Münz *et al.*, 2006*a* and 2006*b*). At present, in Europe, the economic potential of immigrant labour is far from being fully utilised. For example, there is evidence that immigrants are more mobile and flexible than natives in availing themselves of employment opportunities wherever they might exist, and thus have a higher potential to ease the inefficiencies that result from regional disparities within the EU27. Today, though, not all EU nationals are free to work in other EU member states. Allowing all EU nationals access to all national labour markets, and granting third-country nationals residing legally in EU member states for a minimum number of years (between three and five years is a reasonable time frame) the right to do so also could help establish a better integrated and more flexible EU labour market — and thus increase the competitiveness of the overall EU economy.

The recommendations made here seek to provide greater clarity to immigrants and employers regarding the prospects for the long-term relationships they may be considering. There is already some limited momentum in this direction in the EU, with the proposal put forward in 2006 to create an EU "blue card" for highly skilled workers (the card is inspired by the US "green card", though it would offer weaker rights). Also, the Commission's Policy Plan on Legal Migration anticipates a new Directive on highly skilled workers,

ISBN: 978-92-64-03740-3 © OECD 2007

scheduled to be drafted in 2007. While these particular examples concern highly skilled workers, corresponding initiatives are needed to address the mobility of low and medium-skilled migrants. These initiatives, across the skill spectrum, could incorporate the recommendations below.

- Harmonise admission policies across member states

To the greatest degree possible, member states should implement common measures to admit economic immigrants in order to make the EU a more attractive area of immigration.

- Grant the right of effective free movement to certain longer-term immigrants

Member states should allow longer-term holders of permanent residence permits, and of other select categories of visas, the right to move freely and work in any and all EU member states.

Opportunities for Permanent Residence and Citizenship

In choosing where they will go, certain migrants are influenced by their potential right to permanence — for themselves and for their families — and a clear path to citizenship. Likewise, employers tend to invest in certain workers if they have confidence that the additional skills, knowledge and experience these workers acquire will redound to their company over the long-term. At the moment, migrants who qualify as long-term residents, after a minimum of five continuous years' stay in a single EU country, are granted limited mobility rights (European Council Directive, 2003). Even under this Directive, however, member states can deny labour market access to long-term residents. The process of acquiring the rights guaranteed by the Directive is complicated and contingent enough to blunt its effectiveness as a means of attracting skilled migrants.

The first step in establishing well-functioning mobility systems — regardless of the total level of immigration that a country is willing to accept — involves a rational policy governing access to labour markets for third-country nationals and citizens of new EU member states. This rational policy must create more legal channels and more flexible options for migrants' entry and stay. At present, labour-market access regimes, in most EU countries, respond neither to the needs of immigrants nor to those of their employers (Münz *et al.*, 2006*a* and 2006*b*).

   ISBN: 978-92-64-03740-3 © OECD 2007

Opportunities for permanent residence and citizenship should be realised through two policy interventions:

—   granting permanent residence permits for critical workforce needs; and

—   establishing clear paths to citizenship.

With respect to immigrants in critical occupational categories — the categories of which member states are free to define, based on their labour-market needs and/or strategic economic plans — EU member states could grant permanent residence permits. Some immigrants entering critical, pre-defined occupational categories or fulfilling certain criteria (e.g. holders with advanced academic degrees from universities in OECD countries, scientists, engineers or other similarly defined occupational needs) should be granted permanent residence permits from the outset of their stay. Such permits should also apply to immediate family members (spouses and minor children). Finally, spouses of such immigrants should be granted full access to the labour market. While granting such access to spouses might be particularly controversial, the reality of competition for particularly skilled and talented foreigners makes breaking with previous practice essential (See Papademetriou and Yale-Loehr, 1996; Meissner *et al.*, 2006). Concerns about possibly importing workers with the less-needed skills through this channel are not well founded. Family members of foreigners who will tend to benefit from these provisions are likely to share similar social and educational backgrounds making comparisons with current European experiences with family re-unification (usually of unskilled immigrants) invalid.

Establishing clear paths to citizenship means adopting rules for access that are unambiguous, understandable and attainable with reasonable effort. Only those administrative requirements for naturalisation that have specific and legitimate policy purposes, such as public-security ones, or ones that speak to long-term integration purposes such as knowledge of civics and language, should be retained.

These new ways of thinking and acting on mobility will not be easy and must be communicated clearly to all potential clients of the system. Information and recruitment campaigns will be needed to provide prospective migrants with accurate and relevant information about employment opportunities, while reassuring EU citizens that they will suffer no diminution in their access to these opportunities. Offering prospective migrants reliable information about potentially attractive conditions and rights granted in EU member states will be crucial for creating a momentum both for brain inflow to the European Union and brain circulation within it.

ISBN: 978-92-64-03740-3 © OECD 2007

Chapter 4

Migration and Social Cohesion: Enabling Integration

For decades after the Second World War, the belief prevailed in most of Europe that immigration was not a permanent phenomenon. Guest workers were by definition temporary. Refugees often were left in limbo, unable to work, unclear whether and if they could settle permanently. The corollary to this non-immigration presumption was an almost universal failure to develop policies for the integration of immigrants and their descendants. The Netherlands and some of the Nordic countries have been the most noteworthy exceptions in this regard.

In the 1990s, this started to change in many member states. But the scale of the integration challenge financially, politically, and in terms of ideas, is far greater than the resources allocated to it. At the level of the European Union, integration has gained greater prominence, and has been the subject of increasing focus by the European Council and the European Commission. Several relevant directives and communications have been issued since 1999; however, the Commission does not yet have a significant legal basis for common action.

Nonetheless, given that immigrant integration has risen to an exigent challenge for the Union as a whole — affecting not only its economic prospects, but also its social cohesion and its strategy for enlargement — there is clearly an overriding political imperative for action both at the EU level and the individual member state level.

The first imperative is to agree on what integration means, and to liberate the term from ideological debates such as those that surround multiculturalism and/or assimilation. Integration flows from the totality of policies and practices that allow societies to close the gap between the rights, status, and opportunities

ISBN: 978-92-64-03740-3 © OECD 2007

of natives and immigrants (including their descendants). Whether in the realm of education, the job market, housing, health, social services, or political and civic participation, integration efforts should aim to close the persistent opportunity and outcome gaps that marginalise immigrants and undermine social cohesion. The children of immigrants should have the same chances of success at school and in the labour market as the children of natives, and the same likelihood of achieving goals and ambitions.

Nonetheless, charting a course for successful intervention with respect to integration is especially challenging. A broad range of factors — from the reasons for migrating through to conditions in the host society — impact on integration processes. Legal rights are a prerequisite of integration but an insufficient condition for attainment. Migrants face a range of barriers to integration, including restrictions attached to their immigration status, hostile public attitudes and discrimination.

There are, furthermore, status differences within the migrant population, particularly after waves of regularisations and amnesties for illegal or irregular immigrants. Legalisation creates heterogeneities within the migrant group. This leads, in turn, to insider and outsider status with regard to the labour market and the social security system. The status levels are varied, and call for a multiform response from integration policies: some migrants are newly legalised; others remain illegal by choice or because they do not meet the requirements for legalisation; some previously legal immigrants, for various reasons, relapse to illegality; new illegal immigrants in the meantime arrive, hoping for later legalisation; and there are legally resident but clandestinely employed immigrants.

There are also significant differences between and within migrant groups after arrival; such differences are particularly influenced by age and gender. Although some migrants are not disadvantaged relative to the host population, on average migrants are disproportionately disadvantaged in education, housing, health and civic participation (Spencer and Cooper, 2006). The second generation is usually more integrated but can feel excluded or relatively deprived especially if they compare their own opportunities to those of natives, rather than those of extended family members back in their parents' countries of origin (Stark *et al.*, 2006). Identification with their parents' home country or faith is also common and can hinder full integration. Success of integration is difficult to measure because migrants can be well integrated in one sphere but not in another (Spencer and Cooper, 2006).

ISBN: 978-92-64-03740-3 © OECD 2007

Based on these observations, policy makers face four challenges in the realm of integration:

— providing fair and equal access to the labour market at the earliest point in the immigration experience for all migrants and their family members;

— providing access to the educational system, and to specialised language and other classes, at the earliest possible stage in the immigration experience for all family members;

— providing access to the social security system for migrants and their families, contributing according to their ability; and

— enabling the fullest participation of immigrants in the political and social life of their new country, and developing the notion of EU *Multicultural Citizenship* as a long-term holistic framework.

There are many other areas in which action is called for by governments at all levels. Among the areas where sustained policy intervention is required are housing and health care. Innovative approaches must also be developed to address integration challenges specifically linked to gender and faith, while obstacles confronting the second and third generation descendants of immigrants deserve special attention. And as with all public policy, constant monitoring, evaluation and adjustment of policies are essential.

In order for all immigration and integration policies and practices to work more effectively than they do now, it is necessary to engage migrant organisations, associations and networks. This was perhaps the most consistent finding across all the analyses conducted for this project, in nearly every policy field. The scope for action in this regard is summarised in chapter 6.

Fair, Equal and Early Access to the Labour Markets

Employment remains the single most effective prerequisite to integration. A set of studies on the impact of cultural versus economic factors on the integration of migrants in the Netherlands concluded that labour market factors are dominant and have a greater impact than any other policy intervention. Immigrants with jobs are more closely bonded to their host society: they learn the language at higher rates, become embedded in social and cultural networks, and often start their own businesses, building on their work experience. Equally, employed migrants contribute to a positive public image of immigrants (i.e. as hard-working, rather than as a drain on public resources).

ISBN: 978-92-64-03740-3 © OECD 2007

At present, too many obstacles stand in the way of immigrants who seek jobs, and as a result their employment rates are consistently far below those of natives in many (though not all) EU member states at almost all skill levels[1]. This stands in sharp contrast to the situation in the United States, where employment rates of immigrants, especially the unskilled ones, are much higher than those of natives.

In this realm, unlike others related to integration, the necessary policy tools are readily at hand. In many EU countries, the main impediments immigrants face are labour market rigidities, incomplete recognition of degrees and/or inappropriate skills acquired outside of the EU by receiving societies, and discrimination. Breaking down the barriers to employment, therefore, should be the highest priority for European policy makers.

We therefore recommend that member states:

• Facilitate access to their labour markets for all newcomers and their family members from the earliest points in their stay (including asylum seekers who do not enter irregularly, after a reasonable waiting period)

• Introduce better links between training and employment, apprenticeships and life-long training schemes, especially for vulnerable groups, including women, young people, and elderly workers

• Establish common standards for the recognition of degrees and qualifications held by immigrants in partnership with sending countries, including the right to an expeditious appeal to an independent body

• Set up the means by which immigrants can challenge discriminatory behaviour efficiently and without risk to their jobs, including protections for informants and investments in (state-sponsored) strategic litigation

• Strengthen anti-discrimination and anti-racism laws and enforce existing ones, and consider appropriate affirmative action legislation for migrants in all appropriate fields, using as a guide the experience of those member states where affirmative action has been a success[2]

• Create robust job-information systems that provide preferential access to job openings to established residents (to reduce public criticism that immigrants are taking jobs that should have gone to citizens)

• Establish integrated support centres (i.e. "one-stop shops") for immigrants — such as the National Support Centre for Immigration in Portugal run by the High Commission for Immigration and Ethnic Minorities (ACIME) — to allow immigrants to address efficiently all work-related (and other integration) obstacles, with the assistance of an independent advocate

ISBN: 978-92-64-03740-3 © OECD 2007

Education, Language and Adult Learning

Education is an important pathway to integration for children and adults (See Spencer and Cooper, 2006). The social integration of children occurs first and foremost at school, through the acquisition of new skills and through interaction with other pupils. Adult migrants are more likely to encounter this mechanism of integration informally at work or in social settings, though formal introduction programmes can help them acquire some language skills, social orientation, job training and the opportunity to participate in their new community.

Box 4.1 Immigrants, Language, Learning: What Works?

Education systems in most EU countries have not led to the equality sought by integration. Migrant children are disproportionately represented in secondary schools that do not give access to higher education, in special schools, and among those with lower educational attainment (Luciak, 2004). School-based segregation can be marked, leading to children growing up with little contact with members of other communities.

When do immigrants' children succeed in school? Research has identified a wide range of factors as relevant to education outcomes for migrant pupils. The contributing factors include gender, language, age at immigration, socio-economic background, parents' education level, teaching techniques, discrimination, effective induction, and the school's ethos and experience (Spencer and Cooper, 2006; OECD, 2004; OECD, 2006). Authorities need to ensure that the equal right of migrant children to progress in education is not marred by prejudice or by mistaking language difficulties for learning difficulties. It is imperative that migrant children have the opportunity to learn the language of the host country, but it should not be assumed that this will be sufficient to ensure progress at school. It should be noted however that migrants' attachment to their ethnic culture is not found to have a detrimental impact on performance.

Learning the native language of the host country is a key factor in success in education and in the labour market (Van Ours and Veenman, 2001; Reyneri, 2004; O'Leary et al., 2001; Esser, 2006). The OECD's Programme for International Student Assessment study (PISA) of 2004 confirms that poor language knowledge is one of the main factors associated with the disadvantage experienced by students with a foreign background, whether born in the host country or abroad. Results from Belgium, Germany, the Netherlands and Switzerland show that students who do not speak the language of assessment at home are at least 2.5 times more likely to be in the bottom quarter of performance indicators.

Box 4.1 (contd.)

Migrants' propensity to acquire the host country's language is in turn conditioned by their age at immigration, length of stay, parents' background and educational level (Luciak, 2004; Esser, 2006). Linguistic differences, the value of the migrant's own language as a vehicle for worldwide communication, and the migrant's social distance from mainstream society negatively impact language acquisition. Competency in the language of the migrant's country of origin brings no advantage in terms of host-country educational attainment, and conditions that favour the retention of language of origin usually hinder the acquisition of high competency in the host country language (Esser, 2006). Other studies confirm the importance of starting education in the host country at a young age (Spencer and Cooper, 2006).

While retention of migrants' own language might offer little advantage for educational attainment, it might nevertheless boost the migrant's sense of belonging and access to ethnic networks. There are thus conflicting views on the value of own-language teaching at school, historically a feature of education policy in some member states (Vertovec and Wessendorf, 2004). Many parents value teaching minority languages in schools, particularly those who speak such languages at home, but the broader impact of such programmes is less clear (Aarts *et al.*, 2004).

The following recommendations address the critical role of education in integration.

- Provide housing opportunities that allow for better integration

In order to reduce segregation in schools, authorities need to address the housing segregation that is one of its primary causes (Spencer and Cooper, 2006). While some residential segregation benefits migrants, authorities need to ensure that there are opportunities for jobs, education and accommodation elsewhere so that migrants are not trapped in areas cut off from the rest of society: that is, authorities should focus on increased choice, not compulsory dispersal. To facilitate access to suitable housing — which is crucial for health, employment and youth education — authorities can assist through direct provision of accommodation, through providing information and advice, and by using the existing regulatory framework to protect tenants' rights without giving the perception of any special treatment or priority access for migrants (and by countering any misinformation to that effect).

ISBN: 978-92-64-03740-3 © OECD 2007

- Provide host-country language instruction classes for all ages of children, including pre-school age children

All schools should provide language instruction for immigrant children to promote the educational and integration benefits that accompany language acquisition. Pre-school facilities focusing on native-language acquisition should be developed to give those under school age an early start. Crucial to this recommendation is the design of appropriate programmes and policies (Crul, 2007).

- Provide second chances to help secondary students overcome linguistic and cultural disadvantages

School systems that necessitate selecting a scholastic pathway (e.g. choosing to focus the latter years of secondary schooling in the sciences, humanities, social sciences or non-academic curricula for future education) can be disadvantageous for immigrant youth. Children of immigrants usually start school at a linguistic disadvantage. It takes time to make up this disadvantage, and so children in systems with early selection fare worse than they otherwise could (Crul, 2007). There are a number of alternative models to later selection that do not impose fundamental structural change on school systems. The general rule of thumb in all alternative models is to ensure there is a second chance, and that choices made in earlier years will not have lasting effects on future chances in education or the labour force.

- Combat implicit and explicit discrimination that hinders minority access to higher-education institutions

Recruitment and admissions processes at universities should be vetted and reformed to eliminate biases that disadvantage minorities. All admissions should be based on equal access and non-discriminatory policies. Equal access implies that anyone who is eligible to apply to be a student should face no barriers to acceptance in comparison with other eligible applicants[3].

While most literature on integration and education outcomes assesses the role of education for children in schools, there is a growing focus on the role of education in adult integration (Spencer and Cooper, 2006).

Most formal immigrant integration programmes for adults in the European Union primarily consist of education practices in three forms: language training, social orientation courses, and occupational integration measures or vocational training. Integration courses, including language classes, are mandatory in some EU member states. Adult integration programmes, however, can take a collective (i.e. one-size-fits-all) approach, neglecting the differing needs of migrants. The European Commission Handbook on Integration offers detailed guidance on the design and organisation of programmes (European Commission, 2007*a*; see also Spencer and di Mattia, 2004; Urth, 2005).

The available evidence is already sufficient to provide pointers to policy makers. There is clearly value in combining language instruction with social orientation and in tailoring programmes to meet the actual needs of individuals. It is also important to ensure the availability of classes in areas and at times when migrants can attend. Finland is among those countries that create individual integration plans for unemployed migrants, and designates specific actions to help migrants improve their language or other skills. However, introductory courses for migrants in a number of member states are insufficiently tailored to meet the individual needs of migrants and thus have high dropout rates. Some experts propose combining language and orientation components, and using positive rather than negative sanctions to encourage attendance. Where sanctions are used, these should be enforced to retain credibility in the system (Entzinger, 2004). In a number of European countries, the mentoring of adult migrants by longer-established migrants or members of the majority population has value (Sijlbing, 2005; Withol de Wenden, 2005).

For adults in particular, skills-focused education programmes that enable migrants to participate fully in the labour market facilitate social integration as well. Programmes that help to accelerate the acquisition of accreditation in critical occupational categories are important contributors to social integration. Those whose skills are not transferable or whose foreign diplomas are not accepted by the host country cannot obtain jobs that meet their qualifications, thus they do not have the opportunity to integrate with work colleagues with similar educational backgrounds.

Limited access to affordable language tuition and the lack of availability of classes appropriate for migrants' needs thwarts many who want to study. Immigration status can also restrict entitlement to higher and further education, particularly through a requirement to pay international student tuition fees (Griffiths, 2003; Warren, 2006).

ISBN: 978-92-64-03740-3 © OECD 2007

Given this landscape, and the importance to integration of educating adult immigrants, we recommend that EU member states:

- Invest in adult language and introductory programmes, and that this be done in close co-ordination with private-sector actors

It is clear that the success of such programmes hinges on where and when they are offered. For employed adult immigrants, training courses should be offered at the workplace, and should be organised in tandem with employers (the latter can also be offered tax breaks or other incentives). For unemployed immigrants, courses could be made available in their neighbourhoods at low or no cost, perhaps in conjunction with retraining initiatives. And for those immigrants who run households, especially women with school-age children, the most effective locus for language learning and other educational programmes is proving to be in the grounds of the schools their children attend. This has several salutary side benefits, including allowing parents to better monitor their children's educational progress and providing opportunities to connect with the parents of native children (school-based programmes may also help overcome cultural barriers by allowing women to leave the home).

Citizenship, Civic Participation, and EU Multicultural Citizenship

Migration challenges the allegiance of individuals to a single state, as they acquire additional cross-national cultural identities. Acquiring citizenship (nationality) and the formal rights and responsibilities it entails accelerates integration, in addition to being an end in itself.

The path to the full and mutual adaptation of immigrants and their host societies must eventually lead to naturalisation and citizenship. This is the lesson from decades of studies in the traditional countries of immigration, as well as in newer migration destinations. While legal and administrative obstacles have been reduced in many EU member states in recent years, other member states continue to present immigrants (and their descendants) with time-consuming hurdles before they can become full citizens. For the irregular immigrants residing in the European Union, citizenship might not be a possibility for a generation or longer.

ISBN: 978-92-64-03740-3 © OECD 2007

Citizenship can mean more than a set of rights and responsibilities: it includes the legal status of nationality and the right to engage in civil society, but it also involves fundamental issues of identity and belonging. With integration through naturalisation still a distant prospect for millions of immigrants, consideration has been given in several member states to a form of interim pact with immigrants that elaborates on civic engagement and on identity (in France, this takes the form of an "integration contract"). Several EU member states — the Netherlands and Germany among them — have implemented compulsory integration tests as a prerequisite to permanent residency. In 2007, the European Commission is expected to draft a general framework directive defining, among other things, the rights of legally resident economic migrants who are not covered by the existing directive on long-term residents. This will go some way towards realising the notion of civic citizenship, but it will cover only a minority of the Union's immigrants.

A more ambitious agenda for civic and political participation needs to be established in order to accelerate the integration of immigrants. We recommend a series of five measures, presented in order of perceived political viability:

- Ease access to participation in established political structures for all immigrants (political parties, trade unions and civic organisations)

The most obvious of these structures are political parties, which should allow longer-term residents of a country to become members. This is already being done by many parties throughout Europe, which are also investing in establishing offices in predominantly immigrant neighbourhoods. Short of obtaining the franchise, the best means for immigrant voices to be heard is through political parties. Participation in trade unions and civic organisations that leads to more frequent interaction with non-migrants is also essential.

- Invest in training civic leaders from among immigrant ranks

Migrant organisations are the first point of entry to civic engagement for most newcomers. Investments in training immigrants in civic participation, civic leadership and public affairs could play an important role in developing appropriate political and legal policies. Such leaders also can become key interlocutors with local and national governments, and eventually populate government institutions — thus helping the latter more closely resemble society at large.

ISBN: 978-92-64-03740-3 © OECD 2007

- Ensure that public institutions mirror society at large

As in so many areas, the public sector can lead by example, not least by maintaining good practice within its ranks. Governments at the national, regional and local levels should ensure that migrants are employed in the mainstream provision of services to the community, particularly when those services have an integration dimension. This may require a reassessment of procurement practices. Governments are also well positioned to encourage good practice and require integration support to all private bodies they engage as sub-contractors through the use of conditional codes of conduct[4].

- Grant local voting rights after two years to all immigrants legally resident and on a long-term visa

There is no substitute for voting to trigger an immigrant's civic engagement or gain the attention for a community's leadership. With full citizenship requiring a decade or longer for most immigrants, they are denied any formal stake in the democratic process. In several EU member states, immigrants are acquiring the right to vote in municipal and other local elections; the conditions for this vary by place. However, the principle of granting local voting rights is perhaps the single most important one to pursue for the civic engagement of immigrants, short of citizenship.

- Reach political agreement on a more ambitious and holistic vision for citizenship in EU member states

EU Multicultural Citizenship should be the ultimate citizenship goal for all member states and individuals living in the EU (Martiniello, 2006). Integration should be seen as two-way adaptation. This shifts the onus of the integration/adaptation burden from immigrants to all residents of the society, including its major institutions. Principal policy directions that will lead to EU multicultural citizenship include:

— liberalising access to citizenship and allowing for dual citizenship, while eventually envisioning direct access to citizenship in EU member states;

— implementing strong anti-racist and anti-discrimination legislation and policies both at the national and at the EU level, as well as vigorous monitoring (as pursued at the Union level by the European Monitoring Centre on Racism and Xenophobia, and at national levels by such organisations as the Commission for Racial Equality in Britain and the *Centre pour l'égalité des chances et la lutte contre le racisme* in Belgium);

— ensuring equality of treatment of all religions and non-religious beliefs, via the separation of state and religion;

— opening up public education to diverse cultural perspectives, including by incorporating into school curricula courses on cultural diversity and on the contribution of immigration to nation-building and EU-building;

— providing financial support to immigrant associations that help spread knowledge of cultural diversity in a given society and bridge the gap between cultural groups; and

— developing means of involving natives in the adaptation of immigrants.

ISBN: 978-92-64-03740-3 © OECD 2007

Notes

1. For employment and unemployment rates of native and foreign-born populations by level of education in 2003-4, see OECD (2006).

2. Affirmative action legislation for migrants must avoid giving the impression (real or perceived) of discrimination against the native workers; this could defeat the goal of migrants' social integration and thwart social cohesion, particularly if there is high unemployment of native workers.

3. The Institut d'Etudes Politiques in Paris offers a paradigm for how this can be done, through its implementation of Zones d'Education Prioritaires (Priority Education Zones) to recruit students from minority neighbourhoods.

4. An example of this is the Procurement Code of the London Development Authority, which follows the Commission for Racial Equality guide for promoting race equality in public procurement, as well as committing to an increase in the number of minority-owned businesses in its supplier base (see London Development Authority, 2004).

ISBN: 978-92-64-03740-3 © OECD 2007

Chapter 5

Migration and Development: Partnerships for Mobility Management

Migration has profound economic consequences — many of them salutary, others more worrisome — for migrants' home countries (see Katseli *et al.*, 2006*b*). Potentially, migration can have positive effects on the development of sending countries. For example, migration can reduce unemployment, expand development through remittances, improve knowledge and skills, and introduce new technology. It can also, however, aggravate inequality, disrupt family life and social relations, and cripple essential social-service provision. Hence, it is vital to link migration and development policies for more effective management of migration.

EU and EU member-state policies, including those concerned with migration, can have an impact on development in sending countries. Development, in turn, plays a major role in shaping future migration pressures. Linking policies means ensuring coherence across policy domains, such as migration, trade and development co-operation, and finding the synergies and complementarities that will make them work nationally and for the benefit of migrants and their sending countries.

The joint consideration of migration and development co-operation policies can form the basis of genuine migration and development partnerships between sending and receiving countries (and transit countries, where appropriate). These partnerships should exploit the full range of the benefits of co-operation — and the costs of non-cooperation — to pursue more effective management of labour mobility. Sending and receiving countries need to co-ordinate their migration policies with one another and link them to other major domestic policy concerns including employment, vulnerability, security, decent work and/or social cohesion. Our main policy message is that joint consideration of migration and development issues, including development assistance, could improve policies and make difficult compromises easier to handle.

ISBN: 978-92-64-03740-3 © OECD 2007

Linking migration and development policies should not be understood to mean that development assistance can resolve the challenges posed by migration. Aid can help, particularly by enhancing sending countries' capacity to adjust to emigration successfully (through support for infrastructure development, improvements of education and health systems, co-development projects, or support for appropriately designed fellowships and training schemes). However, it is worth pointing out what development assistance should *not* be called upon to provide: stopping or controlling immigration. First, the links from aid to growth are weak and even if aid spurs growth, there is no guarantee that migration will diminish as a result. Second, using development assistance as a bargaining device to extract co-operation in controlling irregular migration, as is sometimes suggested, would be fraught with difficulties. Aside from imposing conditions on aid recipients, low- and middle-income countries, with limited resources, are at least as hard pressed to enforce emigration border controls as EU countries are to enforce immigration border controls. Finally, the principal objective of development assistance should remain poverty eradication. Official Development Assistance should not serve the double goal of poverty reduction and migration control. Given that very little of the low-skill migration to the EU originates from the least-developed countries, redirecting development assistance towards the high-migration middle-income countries in order to influence migration patterns there would run counter to the objective of eradicating the most severe poverty.

Based on the results from this project, policy innovation should be pursued in the following areas:

— EU member states must revisit their migration policies with an eye to ensuring that migrant-sending countries, many of which are developing countries, derive greater benefits from migration flows in a way consistent with member states' development co-operation goals.

— Member states, in the context of their development co-operation policies, must work with developing countries to encourage and assist them to mainstream migration and remittance dimensions into their national development strategies.

— The organisational structures for migration management must be reformed both at the national and EU levels.

— EU and its member states should pursue coherence across different policy domains and generate synergies across migration, trade (including trade in services), security, and development policies; this coherence extends, in line with the European Union's Consensus on Development, to policies affecting employment, decent work and the social dimensions of globalisation.

ISBN: 978-92-64-03740-3 © OECD 2007

Looking at Migration Policies through a Development Lens

To improve migration management and to maximise the positive impact of migration, EU agreements need to address the development impacts of their actions, including those that are derived from recruitment and admission policies, as well as development co-operation policies.

Tackling the Brain Drain

Many EU countries have programmes to facilitate the entry of highly skilled migrants. Indeed, the global competition to attract the best and the brightest is intensifying. The disruption in sending countries from the loss of key personnel, such as health-care workers and educators, can be significant. In addition, the loss accrued from the outlay of public resources invested in training potential emigrants can be very real (see Katseli *et al.*, 2006*a* and 2006*b*). Although a highly educated diaspora could, in principle, provide benefits to the home economy, the evidence for this remains weak and pertains more to upper-middle-income countries, which are better placed to take advantage of technologies transferred from overseas and any fresh skills of a returning diaspora. The reality is, however, that the poorer the country, the higher the fraction of highly educated persons migrating to industrialised countries. How can these trends be influenced to enhance the benefits — the brain gain — while mitigating the costs, especially since EU countries' efforts to attract highly skilled migrants are unlikely to abate?

A number of recommendations related to managing flows of highly skilled migrants were offered in chapter 3 of this report. Following that discussion, we recommend in addition that policies must include a development dimension. This means that:

- Innovative circularity schemes should manage migration flows more effectively without crippling social services in sending countries

Examples already exist of such schemes involving a growing number of professionals (e.g. Japan-Philippines). The EU could expand these schemes to include multi-annual fixed-term contracts to professionals from selected countries to train or work for a limited period in the EU. Such schemes could also be addressed to students and/or postgraduates from developing countries. Under the terms of such agreements, receiving countries could

ISBN: 978-92-64-03740-3 © OECD 2007

commit to help sending countries upgrade and modernise social service-delivery systems (e.g. education, health). Measures that would ensure appropriate training of personnel, staff deployment and replenishment for maintaining social service delivery at the desired level, could also be included.

- EU member states should continue developing guidelines for recruitment of highly skilled workers from developing countries

The United Kingdom has been a pioneer among OECD countries in adopting restraints on the recruitment of health-care workers from developing countries, where their skills are sorely needed. Nevertheless, even there these restraints have proved ineffective in limiting migration of doctors and nurses[1]. Exhorting private-sector employers to recruit ethically is not likely to be more effective. Nevertheless, the joint development of guidelines by European or OECD member countries might offer an alternative mechanism, particularly since multilaterally agreed-upon guidelines governing the recruitment of critically needed workers from developing countries promise more effective restraint than the unilateral measures adopted to date. The OECD, in particular, has frequently been the venue for international deliberation of non-binding guidelines to promote responsible behaviour by member countries; the visibility of the guidelines and peer pressure by other countries can be an effective restraint. Guidelines for the recruitment of critically needed workers in health care and education could both restrict some movements altogether, or more flexibly link circular mobility to training resources.

Organise Recruitment of Low- and Semi-skilled Migrants

Although targeting highly skilled migrants is common in most EU member states, this is not the case with low- and semi-skilled migrants despite the mutual benefits that can be derived from such migration. For sending countries, low- and semi-skilled migration has typically a greater impact on poverty reduction than does emigration of professionals. There are three reasons for this; one that has to do with labour markets and employment, and two that act through the mechanism of remittances. First, when a low-skilled worker leaves the labour market back home it creates a vacancy for an unemployed low-skilled worker who remains behind. Second, the remittances sent home by a low-skilled worker increase the well-being of his or her family and/or community. Third,

ISBN: 978-92-64-03740-3 © OECD 2007

evidence shows that low-skilled workers tend to remit more than high-skilled workers do — as a proportion of their earnings, but sometimes even in absolute terms — especially if they have left their families back home[2].

Despite these potential mutual benefits, effective recruitment of low-skilled migrants is rare. Hence we recommend:

- **EU member states should enter into strategic partnerships with selected migrants' home countries**

Using bilateral schemes to promote circular migration, EU countries can enhance the impact of migration on development of the sending countries. Effective recruitment of temporary or circular migrants in the context of such partnerships might also prove effective in tackling irregular migration. Seasonal or temporary work arrangements under contracts for multi-annual specific service provision and the establishment of clear criteria for return and future re-entry could significantly enhance migrants' incentives to prefer legal channels of entry and honour fixed-term contracts.

- **EU countries must encourage and support regional schemes among developing countries**

As the idea of regional development strategies gains ground, the regional aspects of migration should be considered. Policies to facilitate cross-border regional market integration through improved infrastructure and appropriate visas, including the extension of regional passports, should be adequately considered, especially since much migration is intra-regional. While these accords and agreements will be among non-EU and non-OECD countries, these richer countries can provide resources and build capacity to facilitate negotiations.

A large part of the international migration of less-skilled workers (as well as refugees) is intra-regional, and the migration of the less skilled has the greatest potential to alleviate poverty. A strong economic case can be made for regional level negotiations with an objective of achieving regional level governance. The impacts of migration are regional, not bilateral, and regional arrangements are more likely to include all parties with an interest in more orderly migration management. If bilateral negotiations are more common than regional ones, it is because regional schemes are harder to manage: they will require a strengthening of existing governance structures (e.g. ECOWAS in West Africa, or CAFTA in Central America). Before binding agreements can be reached, the regional partners must agree to political frameworks and legal principles in which those future agreements can be monitored and enforced.

Mobilising and Channelling Remittances for Development

Remittances sent by migrants to families and friends in home countries constitute an important driver of development (See Katseli *et al.*, 2006*b*). The actual amounts that migrants remit depend on economic and financial conditions in both sending and receiving countries; they also depend on the composition of migration flows, as well as the conditions under which the migrants are admitted into the host country and are hence partly determined by OECD-country admission policies. The pro-poor effects associated with remittances are much stronger in the case of low-skilled as opposed to highly skilled migration, especially if highly skilled migrants settle permanently abroad with their families. Low-skilled migrants tend to remit proportionally more and direct their savings to their low-income families, which often remain in the home country.

The reported size of remittances is most likely underestimated. Remittances are often transferred through informal channels rather than banks or formal institutions. The cost of transferring money, while falling rapidly in some migration corridors, remains extremely high for migrants in many OECD countries, particularly in Europe. Furthermore, there are significant differences across countries. For example, the cost of remittances between Europe and West Africa is ten times higher than that between the United States and the Philippines (World Bank, 2006).

We therefore recommend that:

- EU member states take concerted steps to lower the costs of transfers through formal channels while European banks and financial institutions in co-operation with financial institutions in developing countries take the lead in expanding financial services to poor rural communities (where many migrants' families live). This array of initiatives must be a true public-private partnership.

These reforms can be guided by lessons from migration corridors where transfer costs have fallen rapidly (particularly between the United States and Latin America). Such action would facilitate the channelling of remittances in poor communities. Involving migrants and migrant

ISBN: 978-92-64-03740-3 © OECD 2007

associations in such schemes would increase pressure for appropriate services and thus increase the volume of remittances transferred: migrants' networks play an important role in facilitating remittances and promoting their role as a development tool; they act as lobby groups to improve access to financial services for migrants, both in the destination and their country of origin. Moreover they contribute to the collection and dissemination of information on the available channels to transfer their savings to their families back home.

- EU member states must deepen co-development initiatives that harness the resources of transnational diaspora networks to promote development of migrants' home countries.

Co-development, pioneered by France but increasingly explored by many European countries, sees the migrant as a partner in development co-operation. Working with migrants' associations to promote community level infrastructure investment (e.g. schools or roads) is an example of co-development centred on remittances. The concept involves the mobilisation of a wider range of migrants' capital, including human and social capital. We return to these other dimensions of co-development in Chapter 6.

Whether the positive impacts of remittances are diffused from the household level to the whole of the economy depends in large part on how well domestic markets function. If markets are well integrated, increases in local incomes can then be translated into increased trading opportunities with other communities, enhancing growth and employment creation. The availability of infrastructure is similarly a precondition for the diffusion of benefits across regions. Development assistance towards capacity building and infrastructure development in the context of national development strategies can substantially enhance the positive impact of remittances on development.

There is a tremendous void to be filled by private actors in the financial sector of EU member states and in developing countries, one that will likely require public incentives, broadly construed. New branches of financial institutions must spread to remote and rural settings where migrants' families receive remittances. A wide array of new and innovative financial products — such as mortgages for the purchase of a home in El Salvador, secured by earnings from a job in the European Union — could profitably be developed. In the Latin American migration corridor to the United States, some of these niches are being occupied by smaller banks and credit unions, nearly all of them for-profit institutions, and most in partnership with finance institutions in sending countries.

ISBN: 978-92-64-03740-3 © OECD 2007

Integrating International Migration into Development Strategies

The development impact of migration depends not only on migrants' choices, but equally on the capacity of sending countries to adjust successfully to international migration. This capacity depends, in turn, on the active engagement of migrants themselves, as well as on incentives, institutions and policies in sending countries; it can furthermore be strengthened with the support of EU member states.

For countries where emigration is a prominent feature, national development strategies need to bear in mind the effects of migration. These must be considered when determining macro-economic policies, human resource management, education policies and investment incentives, as well as in regional (including South-South) initiatives. In designing such strategies, governments in sending countries need to involve and actively consult migrants and their associations. Engaging diaspora networks in the design of development strategies at home can bring about important political and economic benefits for the sending country

While the bulk of the recommendations in this report are targeted to migrant-receiving countries in Europe, mobility partnerships will call upon migrant-receiving and migrant-sending countries alike to reform policies. Including the effects of migration into national development strategies is first and foremost a recommendation for migrant-sending countries, though the support of migrant-receiving countries can be critical in this effort. In particular, EU member states can use partnership agreements as a vehicle for encouraging non-EU partners to link more productive migration and development policies in migrants' home countries.

For these reasons, we therefore recommend:

- EU member states use partnership arrangements to link recruitment with capacity building and development in sending countries

In particular, a partnership approach could link EU member state migration policies and non-EU countries' human resource development policies. In the presence of emigration, sending countries need to be encouraged to design human resource policies that take into consideration current and projected effects of migration on domestic labour markets, as well as the potential loss of public resources invested in highly skilled emigrants. This implies the provision of sufficient incentives for public sector posts, effective deployment of available personnel and possible restructuring

ISBN: 978-92-64-03740-3 © OECD 2007

of methods of financing higher education. The absorption of highly skilled professionals in developing countries, especially in the health and education sectors, can be substantially improved through investments in service delivery systems, continuous training of personnel and better working conditions. Development assistance can play an important role in such partnership arrangements, by providing resources to migrant-sending economies to strengthen their capacity to adjust. This capacity could include better transport and communication infrastructure to link labour markets within the sending country, and promotion of financial sector development to encourage greater use of formal sector means to transfer remittances.

Overhauling the Organisation of Migration Management

Linking migration and development co-operation policies in the way we have described in the first two sections of this chapter, both at national and supra-national (i.e. EU) levels, will require substantial rethinking of existing institutional set-ups to address the current segmentation of policy competencies across ministries, directorates and organisations. The European Union has explicitly recognised the need for this rethinking: the EU's December 2005 "European Consensus on Development", notably, calls upon the Commission and the EU member states to observe coherence among their policies that affect development. Certainly, migration policies fall into this category. How can this political will be translated into more coherent migration management?

Given the present setting, we recommend:

- At the national level, inter-ministerial initiatives must be established to promote co-ordination of development and migration policies

Introducing inter-ministerial co-ordination mechanisms can significantly improve policy making. Examples of this already exist in the EU. Among EU member states, Sweden's 2003 Government Bill, committing various ministries to greater policy coherence in measures that affect development with annual reporting to Parliament, is probably the most institutionally ambitious initiative. Other EU member states, such as the Netherlands, have also opted for co-ordination mechanisms bringing together development and non-development officials to discuss development impacts of various measures.

- At the level of the Commission, stronger systematic consultations must be put in place across all relevant EC directorates

More regular dialogue across all relevant European Commission directorates (most notably DG Justice, Freedom and Security; DG Employment, Social Affairs and Equal Opportunities; DG Development; and DG External Trade) is necessary to strengthen the development input into the relevant structures responsible for migration policy. Support by a Working Party on Migration, Development, Trade, and the Social Dimension of Globalisation might provide a necessary forum for information exchange, policy consultation and stronger development inputs on migration policy making.

Coherence of Policies for More Effective Management

Some of the key factors shaping employment creation, economic development, and even security at home lie beyond the control of the migrants' home countries. External factors — including EU country policies (e.g. in agriculture, trade, environment or security), but also changing world terms of trade, climate swings, or even violence instigated by neighbouring states — impinge upon living conditions that alter pressures to migrate internationally. Nevertheless, the development strategies chosen by migrants' home countries can play a major role in mitigating risks and seizing opportunities for development. This can be facilitated if migration, trade, investment, development assistance and related aspects of employment, decent work and the social dimensions of globalisation are jointly addressed at the national, regional and global levels (See Dayton-Johnson and Katseli, 2006; Katseli *et al.*, 2006a).

- EU trade policy should be crafted with attention to its impact upon labour mobility

Being able to export products that make intensive use of low-skilled labour is a critical strategy for accelerated growth and the principal rationale for opening to trade. Expansion of such export industries will in some cases affect migration flows. Such a growth strategy is complicated by the trade policies of the EU and its member states, however. The use of agricultural subsidies by many of the industrialised countries that would, for example,

ISBN: 978-92-64-03740-3 © OECD 2007

depress world prices for agricultural products would also be likely to hurt living conditions in countries that are exporters of cash crops, possibly exacerbating migration pressures (see Suwa-Eisenmann and Verdier, 2006; Xenogiani, 2006). While the impacts of such policies on potential migrants vary within and across developing countries, this example illustrates that the impacts of EU trade (including, notably, trade in services), migration and development policies on specific low- and middle-income developing countries need to be considered alongside migration policy making.

- EU and EU member states' security policies must recognise the broad nature of insecurity and the relationship between insecurity and labour mobility

An EU agenda on security and development should address the links between development, migration and security. EU policies and programmes could explicitly aim to address the various sources of insecurity (e.g. inability to access strategic assets, access to food and water, large market volatility or failed institutional set ups) that often cause people to emigrate and which hamper development. Improving access to land and water assets, supporting agricultural extension programmes and irrigation infrastructure, and promoting institutional capacity-building, as well as appropriate land titling and regulatory modernisation, are only a few examples of policy priorities that could significantly enhance security in the countries of origin and stem the desire for relocation.

Notes

1. Findlay (2006) assesses the British National Health Service's record in banning recruitment from some developing countries.

2. The extensive empirical evidence on the relationship between the skills profile of migrants and the impact back home of their emigration is summarised and synthesised in Katseli *et al.* (2006) and in OECD (2007*a*).

ISBN: 978-92-64-03740-3 © OECD 2007

Chapter 6

Encouraging Migrants' Networks

Migrants need to become partners in policy making and policy implementation. Migrant organisations provide individuals with connections, information, access to services and an opportunity to develop their skills (Rindoks *et al.*, 2006). They can also be empowering by helping to imbue a sense of status and shared identity, which helps in campaigns to influence local and national policies. Strong migrant organisations usually enhance, rather than prevent, links with the mainstream political system.

Migrant networks can help immigrants find jobs and integrate economically. Migrant organisations can often play a leadership role within social networks by providing guidance and services to immigrants. While some organisations provide assistance in filing documentation for family reunification or citizenship, others offer second-language programmes and vocational training to upgrade job skills. By partnering with local schools, community colleges, hospitals and vocational training centres, migrant organisations provide meaningful services to their clients.

Both social and organisational networks can help immigrants contribute to the economy. As immigrants settle, form communities and organise among themselves, they create social networks. These networks allow immigrants to pool resources for establishing small and medium-sized enterprises. They can provide access to financial capital through informal channels (as in the well-documented examples of Chinese, Japanese and West African diasporas), or lower business costs through information sharing and facilitating labour supply (as in the case of German employers who rely on referrals from current Polish employees to extend job offers to new immigrants). Many immigrants commonly rely on referrals from friends or relatives in their social networks or on organisational networks to secure employment. This is a particularly valuable role of networks given the difficulty in finding jobs through formal routes.

ISBN: 978-92-64-03740-3 © OECD 2007

Social networks can also spur trade. High demand for home products and services among immigrants has encouraged many immigrants to start or invest in businesses specialising in such trade and exchange. In doing so, such immigrant entrepreneurs use their understanding of the needs of their communities to supply products and services that effectively respond to local needs and demands. Hence, social networks strengthen supply chain production networks and business links not only within communities and countries but across national borders. As such, social networks in countries of immigration can help expand the economies of developing countries through increased trade remittances, and knowledge transfers.

Finally, migrant and diaspora networks can be important partners in development co-operation. Traditionally, OECD country governments and international organisations such as the International Organization for Migration (IOM) have engaged diaspora networks to facilitate the return of migrants — by means of assisted voluntary return (AVR) programmes — and to assist them in their reintegration in their home countries (de Haas, 2006). Recent initiatives have started engaging migrants' networks as development partners in more imaginative ways. In place of encouraging voluntary return, diaspora networks are being increasingly mobilised to foster a kind of virtual return. Initiatives of this kind focus on repatriation of skills and resources, but not necessarily of the migrants themselves. Such a repatriation of resources could be powerfully catalysed by remittances. One example of this is the *Tres por uno* programme in Zacatecas State, Mexico, which had the state and federal governments matching each remittance dollar sent from the United States (Iskander, 2005). In addition to endorsing the idea of governments matching remittance funds, the European Investment Bank (EIB), for example, recommends that banking systems offer banking services specifically targeted at migrants (including mortgage products, remittance-tailored bank accounts and investments funds) in order to channel remittances into productive investments (de Haas, 2006).

Co-development projects, pioneered by France, while still relatively small in number and scale, include projects in the home countries involving migrants who live in EU member states (in particular business people, academics, health personnel and engineers). Migrants are encouraged to promote commercial activities or implement social development projects (building schools or health centres) or lend their expertise to their home country. Moreover, the concept of co-development also includes helping migrants to direct their savings better towards productive investment in their countries of origin. This concerns especially the transfer of monies as well as strengthening the capacities of micro-credit institutions. As such, an increasing concern of co-development is how to catalyse and amplify the effects of social investments made with remittances (OECD, 2007*a*).

ISBN: 978-92-64-03740-3 © OECD 2007

Given the positive impact of migrant organisations and networks along the entire spectrum of the migration experience — from helping recruit qualified labour in home countries to easing integration, and spurring economic growth in both the home and host societies — we recommend that EU member states:

- Provide substantial funding to support migrant organisations and networks

In making grants to organisations and networks, however, authorities must be vigilant in ensuring that they are not seen to be playing favourites; independent mechanisms for the disbursal of financial support should be established. Successful examples of such initiatives include the Vienna Integration Office, which funds networking activities of migrant associations.

- Incorporate migrant organisations into the policy-making process

No serious policy can be developed without the active participation of migrants themselves. To this end, at the EU level, the European Commission should create a permanent contact group of migrant associations' religious leaders and experts to advise the Commission on all policies related to managing the new mobility system. The Commission should also offer training and leadership courses for key personnel in national organisations, thus better enabling them to organise their communities to participate in policy-making processes. Similar initiatives should be taken at the national, regional and local levels.

- Deepen co-development initiatives that work with migrant organisations to implement development co-operation policy

One of the characteristics of migrant organisations that make them well suited to enhance economic and social integration also makes them good partners for development policy: namely, superior information and knowledge about conditions (economic, social or otherwise) in their home country. Co-development policies that are not fundamentally aimed at encouraging return migration are a promising mechanism for enhancing the positive development impacts of international migration.

ISBN: 978-92-64-03740-3 © OECD 2007

Much of the challenge that besets migration policy making — and which, more generally, stands in the way of realising greater gains from migration — stems from difficult trade-offs among policy objectives. These trade-offs are highlighted in the titles of the chapters of this report: migration versus high employment; migration versus social cohesion; migration versus development. The analysis underlying this report suggests that such trade-offs are sometimes more apparent than real. For example, migration flows often ameliorate labour market problems rather than accentuate them. To take another example: migration flows, effectively managed, can contribute to international economic development. The aim of this final chapter has been to show how migrants' networks, both formal and informal, can likewise be mobilised to ease these trade-offs: Migrants' networks can facilitate labour-market adjustment, integration of newcomers and the effectiveness of development co-operation.

ISBN: 978-92-64-03740-3 © OECD 2007

Annex

List of Outputs

1) Evaluative Critical Reviews

1. *The Costs and Benefits of European Immigration,* by Rainer Münz, Thomas Straubhaar, Florin Vadean and Nadia Vadean.

2. *Social Integration of Migrants in Europe: A Review of the European Literature 2000-2006,* by Sarah Spencer and Betsy Cooper.

3. *Gaining from Migration: What Works in Networks? Examining Economically Related Benefits Accrued from Greater Economic Linkages, Migration Processes, and Diasporas,* by Aimee Rindoks, Rinus Penninx and Jan Rath.

4. *Effects of Migration on Sending Countries: What Do We Know?,* by Louka T. Katseli, Robert E.B. Lucas and Theodora Xenogiani.

2) Flagships

Policy Coherence for Development: Migration and Developing Countries, Development Centre Perspectives (OECD, 2007*a*).

3) Policy Briefs

5. *New Migration Thinking for a New Century,* by Demetrios G. Papademetriou and Doris Meissner.

6. *Policies for Migration and Development: A European Perspective,* by Louka T. Katseli, Robert E.B. Lucas and Theodora Xenogiani. Published as *OECD Development Centre Policy Brief No. 30.*

7. *What are the Migrants' Contributions to Employment and Growth? A European Approach,* by Rainer Münz, Thomas Straubhaar, Florin Vadean and Nadia Vadean.

8. *What are the Requirements for Migrants' Effective Integration?,* by Marco Martiniello.

ISBN: 978-92-64-03740-3 © OECD 2007

4) Case Studies

9. *Costs and Benefits of Migration for Central European Countries*, by Marek Okólski, Warsaw University, Poland.

10. *Seasonal Migration in Poland*, by O. Stark, Universities of Bonn, Klagenfurt, and Vienna; Warsaw University; ESCE Economic and Social Research Center, Cologne; C. Eisenstadt and S. Fan, Lingnan University and University of Klagenfurt; E. Kepinska, Warsaw University; and M. Micevska, University of Klagenfurt, ESCE Economic and Social Research Center, Cologne.

11. *Costs and Benefits of Migration for Albania*, by Eugenia Markova, London School of Economics and Political Sciences, UK.

12. *Costs and Benefits of Migration for Bulgaria*, by Eugenia Markova, London School of Economics and Political Sciences, UK.

13. *Costs and Benefits of Migration for India*, by Devesh Kapur, University of Pennsylvania, USA.

14. *Gaining From Migration: A Comparative Analysis and Perspective on How Sending and Receiving Countries can Gain from Migration. Turkey Case Study*, by Ahmet Icduygu, Koc University, Turkey.

15. *Migration in Greece*, by Jennifer Cavounidis, IMEPO, Nicolas Glytsos, KEPE and Theodora Xenogiani, OECD Development Centre.

5) Related Case Studies by the Development Centre

16. *Moldova (Aid and Migration)*, by Daniela Borodak.

17. *Mali (Aid and Migration)*, by Flore Gubert and Marc Raffinot.

18. *Guatemala/Honduras: Migration and Trade*, by Samuel Freije.

19. *Ghana: Aid and Migration,* by Peter Quartey.

20. *Morocco: Trade and Migration*, by Lionel Fontagné, Nicolas Péridy and Bachir Hamdouche.

21. *Ecuador: Migration and FDI*, by Iliana Olivié, Alicia Sorroza and Hugo Jácome.

ISBN: 978-92-64-03740-3 © OECD 2007

Bibliography

AARTS, R., G. EXTRA and K. YAĞMUR (2004), "Multilingualism in The Hague" *in* G. EXTRA and K. YAĞMUR (eds.), *Urban Multilingualism in Europe: Immigrant Minority Languages at Home and School*, pp. 193-220, Multilingual Matters, Clevedon.

ABELLA, M. (2006), "Policies and Best Practices for Management of Temporary Migration", UN/POP/MIG/SYMP/2006/03, UN International Symposium on International Migration and Development, Turin.

BORODAK, D. (2006), "Migration et Développement Économique en Moldavie", OECD Development Centre, Paris. For access information go to: www.oecd.org/dev/migration.

CAVOUNIDIS, J., N. GLYTSOS and T. XENOGIANI (2002), "Migration in Greece", OECD Development Centre, Paris. For access information go to: www.oecd.org/dev/migration.

CRUL, M. (2007), *Pathways to Success for the Children of Immigrants*, Migration Policy Institute, Washington, D.C.

DAYTON-JOHNSON, J. and L.T. KATSELI (2006), "Aid, Trade and Migration: Policy Coherence for Development", *Policy Brief* No. 28, OECD Development Centre, Paris.

DE HAAS, H. (2006), "Engaging Diasporas: How Governments and Development Agencies Can Support Diaspora Involvement in the Development of Origin Countries", Study prepared for Oxfam Novib, The Hague.

ENTZINGER, H. (2004), *Integration and Orientation Courses in a European Perspective*. Expert report written for the Sachverständigenrat für Zuwanderung und Integration, Rotterdam. Available at: http://www.bamf.de/template/zuwanderungsrat/expertisen/expertise_entzinger.pdf.

ESSER, H. (2006), *Migration, Sprache, Integration*, AKI-Forschungsbilanz 4. Arbeitsstelle interkulturelle Konflikte und gesellschaftliche Integration (Wissenschaftszentrum Berlin für Sozialforschung), Berlin. Available at: www.aki.wz-berlin.de

EUROPEAN COMMISSION (2004), "Proposal for a Directive of the European Parliament and of the Council on Services in the Internal Market" (presented by the Commission), Commission of the European Communities, [SEC (2004) 21], Brussels, 13.1.2004, COM(2004) 2 final.

EUROPEAN COMMISSION (2005*a*), "Policy Plan on Legal Migration", COM(2005) 669 final, Available at: http://eur-lex.europa.eu/LexUriServ/site/en/com/2005/com2005_0669en01.doc

EUROPEAN COMMISSION (2005*b*), "A Common Agenda for Integration: Framework for the Integration of Third-Country Nationals in the European Union". Available at: http://europa.eu.int/eur-lex/lex/LexUriServ/site/en/com/2005/com2005_0389en01.pdf.

EUROPEAN COMMISSION (2005*c*), "Migration and Development", (COM/2005/0390) available at: http://eur-lex.europa.eu/LexUriServ/LexUriServ.do?uri=CELEX:52005DC0390:EN:NOT.

EUROPEAN COMMISSION (2007*a*), *Handbook on Integration for Policy-Makers and Practitioners.* Directorate-General for Justice, Freedom and Security. Available at: http://ec.europa.eu/justice_home/doc_centre/immigration/integration/doc/2007/handbook_2007_en.pdf.

EUROPEAN COMMISSION (2007*b*), "On Circular Migration and Mobility Partnerships Between the European Union and Third Countries", Communication from the Commission to the European Parliament, the Council, the European Economic and Social Committee and the Committee of the Regions, COM(2007)248. Available at: http://eur-lex.europa.eu/LexUriServ/site/en/com/2007/com2007_0248en01.pdf

EUROPEAN COUNCIL (TAMPERE) (1999), "Tampere European Council, 15 and 16 October 1999, Presidency Conclusions".

EUROPEAN COUNCIL (2003), "Status of Third-country Nationals Who are Long-term Residents", European Council Directive 2003/109/EC.

EUROPEAN COUNCIL (2004*a*), "The Hague Programme: Strengthening Freedom, Security and Justice in the European Union".

EUROPEAN COUNCIL (2004*b*), "Conditions of Admission of Third-country Nationals for the Purposes of Studies, Pupil Exchange, Unremunerated Training or Voluntary Service", European Council Directive 2004/114/EC.

EUROPEAN COUNCIL (2005). "Admission and Residence of Researchers from Third Countries", European Council Directive 2005/71/EC.

EUROSTAT (2005), *European Labour Force Survey,* ad hoc modules.

FINDLAY, A.M. (2006), "Brain Strain and Other Social Challenges Arising from the UK's Policy on Attracting Global Talent", *in* C. KUPTSCH and P.E. Fong (eds.), *Competing for Global Talent,* International Institute for Labour Studies, International Labour Office, Geneva, and Wee Kim Wee Centre, Singapore Management University.

FONTAGNÉ, L. and N. PÉRIDY (2006), "Morocco: Trade and Migration", unpublished manuscript, OECD Development Centre, Paris. For access information, go to: www.oecd.org/dev/migration.

ISBN: 978-92-64-03740-3 © OECD 2007

Freije, S. (2006a), "Migration and Trade Between Mexico and Central America: Policy Coherence for Development: Mexico/Central America Case Study", OECD Development Centre, Paris. For access information, go to: www.oecd.org/dev/migration.

Freije, S. (2006b), "Guatemala/Honduras: Migration and Trade", unpublished manuscript, OECD Development Centre, Paris.

Glytsos, N. (2005), "Stepping from Illegality to Legality and Advancing towards Integration: The Case of Immigrants in Greece", *International Migration Review*, Vol. 39, Winter, pp. 819-840.

Griffiths, D. (2003), *English Language Training for Refugees in London and the Regions*, Online Report 14/03. Home Office, London.

Gubert, F. and M. Raffinot (2006), "Mali: Aid and Migration", unpublished manuscript, OECD Development Centre, Paris. For access information, go to: www.oecd.org/dev/migration.

Hamdouche, B. (2006), "Les Migrations: une analyse économique", unpublished manuscript. For access information, go to: www.oecd.org/dev/migration.

Holzmann, R., J. Koettl and T. Chernetsky (2005), "Portability Regimes of Pension and Health Care Benefits for International Migrants: An Analysis of Issues and Good Practices", Social Protection Discussion Series No. 0519, World Bank, Washington, D.C.

Icduygu, A. (2006), *Gaining From Migration: A Comparative Analysis and Perspective on How Sending and Receiving Countries can Gain from Migration. Turkey Case Study*, OECD Development Centre, Paris. For access information, go to: www.oecd.org/dev/migration.

Iskander, N. (2005), "Social Learning as a Productive Project: The *Tres por uno* (Three for one) Experience at Zacatecas, Mexico" *in Migration, Remittances and Development* 249-264, OECD, Paris.

Jandl, M. (2004), "The Estimation of Illegal Migration in Europe", *Studi Emigrazione/ Migration Studies*, Vol. XLI, No. 153, March 2004, pp. 141-155.

Kapur, D. (2007), *Costs and Benefits of Migration for India*, unpublished manuscript, OECD Development Centre, Paris. For access information, go to: www.oecd.org/dev/migration.

Katseli, L. (2007), "EU Policy Coherence on Security and Development: A New Agenda for Research and Policy Making", *in* H.G. Brauch (ed.), *Institutional Security Concepts Revisited for the 21st Century*, Chapter 60, Springer Verlag, Berlin.

Katseli, L., R. Lucas and T. Xenogiani (2006a), "Policies for Migration and Development: A European Perspective", *Policy Brief* No. 30, OECD Development Centre, Paris.

Katseli, L., R. Lucas and T. Xenogiani (2006b), "Effects of Migration on Sending Countries: What Do We Know?", *Working Paper* No. 250, OECD Development Centre, Paris.

ISBN: 978-92-64-03740-3 © OECD 2007

London Development Authority (2004), Procurement Code. Available at: http://www.lda.gov.uk/server/show/ConWebDoc.316

Luciak, M. (2004), *Migrants, Minorities and Education. Documenting Discrimination and Integration in 15 member states of the European Union*, European Monitoring Centre on Racism and Xenophobia, Luxembourg.

Markova, E. (2006a), "Gaining from Migration: Albania Case Study", OECD Development Centre, Paris. For access information, go to: www.oecd.org/dev/migration.

Markova, E. (2006b), "Gaining from Migration: Bulgaria Case Study", OECD Development Centre, Paris. For access information, go to: www.oecd.org/dev/migration.

Martin, P. (2006), "Managing Labour Migration: Temporary Worker Programmes for the 21st Century", UN/POP/MIG/SYMP/2006/07, UN International Symposium on International Migration and Development, Turin. Available at: http://www.un.org/esa/population/migration/turin/index.html.

Martiniello, M. (2006), "What are the Requirements for Migrants' Effective Integration?", unpublished manuscript, OECD Development Centre, Paris. For access information, go to: www.oecd.org/dev/migration.

Meissner, D., D.Meyers, D.Papademetriou and M. Fix (2006), *Immigration and America's Future: A New Chapter*, Migration Policy Institute, Washington, D.C.

Münz, R., T. Straubhaar, F. Vadean and N. Vadean (2006a), "The Costs and Benefits of European Immigration", OECD Development Centre, Paris; and Hamburg Institute of International Economics, Hamburg. For access information, go to: www.oecd.org/dev/migration.

Münz, R., T. Straubhaar, F. Vadean and N. Vadean (2006b), "What are the Migrants' Contributions to Employment and Growth? A European Approach", Paper prepared for the OECD Development Centre, Paris. For access information, go to: www.oecd.org/dev/migration.

OECD (2004), *Learning for Tomorrow's World - First Results from PISA 2003*, OECD, Paris.

OECD (2005), Database on Foreign-born and Expatriates, OECD, Paris.

OECD (2006), *International Migration Outlook*, OECD, Paris.

OECD (2007a), *Policy Coherence for Development: Migration and Developing Countries*, Development Centre Perspectives, OECD Development Centre, Paris.

OECD (2007b), *International Migration Outlook*, OECD, Paris.

Okólski, M. (2006), "Costs and Benefits of Migration for Central European Countries", OECD Development Centre, Paris. For access information, go to: www.oecd.org/dev/migration.

ISBN: 978-92-64-03740-3 © OECD 2007

O'leary, N., P. Murphy, S.J. Drinkwater and D. Blackaby (2001), "English Language Fluency and the Ethnic Wage Gap for Men in England and Wales", *Economic Issues* 6, No. 1, pp. 21-32.

Olivié, I., A. Sorroza and H. Jácome (2006), "Ecuador: Migration and FDI", unpublished manuscript, OECD Development Centre, Paris. For access information, go to: www. oecd.org/dev/migration.

Papademetriou, D. and D. Meissner (2006), "New Migration Thinking for a New Century", OECD Development Centre, Paris. For access information, go to: www. oecd.org/dev/migration.

Papademetriou, D. and S. Yale-Loehr (1996), *Balancing Interests: Rethinking the U.S. Selection of Skilled Immigrants,* Carnegie Endowment for International Peace and The Brookings Institution, Washington, D.C.

Quartey, P. (2006), "Migration, Aid and Development – A Ghana Country Case Study", OECD Development Centre, Paris. For access information, go to: www.oecd. org/dev/migration.

Rannveig Agunias, D. and K. Newland (2007), "Circular Migration and Development: Trends, Policy Routes, and Ways Forward", *Policy Brief,* Migration Policy Institute, Washington, D.C. Available at: http://www.migrationpolicy.org/pubs/MigDevPB_041807.pdf.

Reyneri, E. (2004), "Education and the Occupational Pathways of Migrants in Italy", *Journal of Ethnic and Migration Studies* 30, No. 6. pp. 1145-62.

Rindoks, A., R. Penninx and J. Rath (2006), "Gaining from Migration: What Works in Networks? Examining Economically Related Benefits Accrued from Greater Economic Linkages, Migration Processes and Diasporas", OECD Development Centre, Paris. For access information, go to: www.oecd.org/dev/migration.

Sijlbing, I. (2005), "The Netherlands", *in* R. Süssmuth and W. Weidenfeld (eds.), *Managing Integration: The European Union's Responsibility Toward Immigrants,* the Bertelsmann Foundation and the Migration Policy Institute, Washington, D.C.

Spencer, S. and B. Cooper, (2006), "Social Integration of Migrants in Europe: A Review of the European Literature 2000-2006", OECD Development Centre, Paris. For access information, go to: www.oecd.org/dev/migration.

Spencer, S. and A. Di Mattia (2004), "Introductory Programmes and Initiatives for New Migrants in Europe", *Policy Brief,* in Ministerial Integration Conference on "Turning Principles into Actions", pp. 9-31, Migration Policy Institute and The Netherlands' Ministry of Justice, Groningen, 9-11 November.

Sriskandarajah, D. and C. Drew, (2006), *Brits Abroad: Mapping the Scale and Nature of British Emigration,* Institute for Public Policy Research, London.

ISBN: 978-92-64-03740-3 © OECD 2007

STARK, O., S. FAN, E. KEPINSKA and M. MICEVESKA (2006), "Seasonal Migration", OECD Development Centre, Paris. For access information, go to: www.oecd.org/dev/migration.

SUWA-EISENMANN, A. and T. VERDIER (2006), "The Coherence of Trade Flows and Trade Policies with Aid and Investment Flows", *Working Paper* No. 254, OECD Development Centre, Paris.

UNCTAD (2003), *Increasing the Participation of Developing Countries through Liberalization of Market Access in GATS Mode 4 for Movement of Natural Persons Supplying Services*, United Nations Conference on Trade and Development, Geneva.

UNITED NATIONS (2006), *Trends in Total Migrant Stock: the 2005 Revision*, United Nations, POP/DB/MIG/REV.2005. Data in digital form available from: http://esa.un.org/migration

URTH, H. (2005), "Draft Synthesis Report on Policies Concerning the Integration of Immigrants", *in* R. SÜSSMUTH and W. WEIDENFELD (eds.), *Managing Integration: The European Union's Responsibility Toward Immigrants*, the Bertelsmann Foundation and the Migration Policy Institute, Washington, D.C.

VAN OURS, J.C. and J. VEENMAN (2001), "The Educational Attainment of Second Generation Immigrants in the Netherlands", discussion paper No. 297, Institute for the Study of Labour, Bonn.

VERTOVEC, S. and S. WESSENDORF (2004), *Migration and Cultural, Religious, and Linguistic Diversity in Europe: An Overview of Trends and Issues*, International Migration, Integration, and Social Cohesion, Amsterdam.

WARREN, S. (2006), "Integration of New Migrants: Education", *in* S. SPENCER (ed.), *New Migrants and Refugees: Review of the Evidence on Good Practice*, Home Office/Compas, London.

WINTERS, L.A., T.L. WALMSLEY, Z.K. WANG and R. GRYNBERG (2003), "Negotiating the Temporary Movement of Natural Persons: An Agenda for the Development Round", *The World Economy*, Vol. 26 (8), pp.1137-1162.

WITHOL DE WENDEN, C. (2005), "A French Perspective", *in* R. SÜSSMUTH and W. WEIDENFELD (eds.), *Managing Integration: The European Union's Responsibility Toward Immigrants*, The Bertelsmann Foundation and the Migration Policy Institute, Washington, D.C.

WORLD BANK (2006), *Global Economic Prospects*, World Bank, Washington, D.C.

XENOGIANI, T. (2006), "Policy Coherence for Development: A Background Paper on Migration Policy and its Interactions with Policies on Aid, Trade and FDI", *Working Paper* No. 249, OECD Development Centre, Paris.

ISBN: 978-92-64-03740-3 © OECD 2007